BUDDHISM
in a *foreign* land

ROBERT MANN is assistant teacher at the House of Inner Tranquillity, a Buddhist meditation centre in Wiltshire, England. He is co-author of *Buddhist Character Analysis*.

BUDDHISM
in a *foreign* land

Robert Mann

AUKANA
BRADFORD ON AVON

First published in 1996

Aukana Trust
9 Masons Lane
Bradford on Avon
Wiltshire
BA15 1QN

The Aukana Trust is a registered charity (No 326938)

Typeset in Bembo 11/13.5 by LP&TS Publishing, Somerton
Printed in Great Britain by Redwood Books, Trowbridge

Cover printed by Devenish & Co, Bath
Cover photograph © Robert Mann

A catalogue record for this book is available from the British Library

ISBN 0-9511769-6-X

ACKNOWLEDGEMENTS

The author would like to thank **Rose Youd**
for her invaluable help with editing this collection of talks
and the **Pali Text Society** for permission to quote from
their copyright translations of the Pali Canon.

CONTENTS

Buddhism in a Foreign Land

A reporter once suggested to a Thai ex-government minister that Buddhism was almost terminally degenerate, with Buddhist monks giving advice on topics like astrology, marriage and lottery tickets.

The minister replied, somewhat enigmatically, that Buddhism in Thailand was like a martini. When pressed to explain, he added that many of the religious customs in his native land were a mish-mash of animist and Hindu beliefs - these were the vermouth and bitters. Get rid of all the superficial irrelevancies and you were left with the purity of the Buddha's teaching - that was the neat gin.

★ ★ ★

Some claim that Buddhism is now the fastest growing religion in Europe. Whether or not that is true, there is certainly tremendous interest in the Buddhist path. When my teacher taught in London in the late 1960's, you could count the number of Buddhist meditation centres in the country on the fingers of one hand (and still have fingers to spare). Within a generation, the number of Buddhist groups in Britain has mushroomed.

Today there are groups representing all aspects of Buddhism. There are groups with strong links with traditional oriental schools – Tibetan, Thai, Japanese; there are eclectic groups, combining a variety of approaches; there are academically inclined groups whose major interest is the study of the traditional scriptures; there are groups whose main emphasis falls on the practical application of the Buddhist path.

One such group is the House of Inner Tranquillity, a meditation centre in Wiltshire which was founded in 1980 by Alan and Jacqui James (Jacqui died in 1989). The course of training at the centre is solidly based in the Buddha's teaching as recorded in the Pali Canon (the collection of the original discourses of the Buddha which forms the basis of Theravada Buddhism). It emphasises meditation, service and study; it encourages commitment to the path and hard work. Because it doesn't provide any of the exotic trappings often associated with Buddhism, for some it can seem a bit too much like neat gin.

I've been a student at the House of Inner Tranquillity since 1980 and assistant teacher since 1987. These talks – given by a western student of a western teacher, who was himself taught by a westerner – could be described as third-generation western Buddhism.

* * *

The Buddha's path is established in the West (albeit on a small scale), and there is a growing number of groups completely independent of the umbilical cord that originally connected the teaching to the East. However, it is almost inevitable that an ancient, eastern way such as the path of the Buddha includes certain things that are culturally alien to modern western society.

Indeed, one initial difficulty the West has encountered in relation to Buddhism is an uncertainty about exactly how to classify it. Some have described it as a religion, others as a philosophy. Neither of these labels is accurate. A case could be made for describing the various cultural accretions as a religion but the Buddha's teaching itself has none of the concerns of a religion – it is free of all concepts of worship or a creator god. And neither is it a philosophy, as the West uses the term, because it is essentially pragmatic and free of speculation.

The Buddha's teaching is simply a way to truth, a practical guide to the overcoming of distress. And yet due to our Judaeo-Christian conditioning we often relate to the teaching as if it were a system of morality; and our cultural bias towards intellectuality encourages us to regard the Buddha's description of reality as just another intriguing theory.

When it comes to the actual practice of meditation, the tendency towards intellectualisation can be a major problem. The essence of the Buddha's path to enlightenment is simple observation. Meditation is all about developing the capacity to pay attention to what is actually present in the moment (as opposed to what we think is present in the moment). Meditators attached to intellectuality typically spend a few seconds paying attention to objects coming and going and then several minutes thinking about the relevance and/or meaning of what they have just seen.

The idea that we can think our way to truth is a serious obstacle. Someone attached to this idea is always trying to interpret experience rather than just observing it.

Buddhist meditation is, in essence, very, very simple. The Buddha said that we suffer because we ignore the true nature of reality. Most critically, we ignore three basic facts of existence. We ignore the transient nature of things, choosing instead to see a world of stability and permanence. We ignore unsatisfactoriness, choosing to hold on to the belief that certain things will bring us complete, lasting happiness. And we ignore what the Buddha called the *anatta* nature of things.

Anatta literally means non-self. When we ignore this mark, we assume that the world is made up of lasting, independent entities. We ignore interdependence and interconnectedness, choosing instead to interpret life in terms of separation, ownership and control. At its crudest level, this ignorance of *anatta* means we respond to life as if we were the centre of the universe.

The Buddha went on to say that this ignorance is chosen. We may be unaware that we ignore reality but, whether it's conscious or not, ignorance inevitably leads to suffering. Reducing ignorance reduces suffering; further, the eradication of ignorance is the eradication of suffering.

Insight meditation (*vipassana* in Pali) is the most direct method of reversing ignorance. *Vipassana* is the systematic training in seeing things as transient (*anicca*), as ultimately unsatisfactory (*dukkha*) and as non-self, not being ownable or controllable (*anatta*). These three aspects (or marks as they are traditionally called) are themselves interconnected. Rather than being three disparate qualities, they could be more accurately described as holographic - true insight into any one of the marks brings understanding of all three.

In practice, the meditation is usually centred around the observation of transience - for no other reason than that this is generally the most accessible of the three marks. Meditation involves turning the mind back, time and time again, to the observation of transience. Everything of which we become aware, in mind and body, is observed to arise and pass away.

The process is completely non-intellectual. Nothing that arises in the practice, no matter how portentous, needs to be interpreted.

Learning to meditate entails a simplification of our mental universe. We start to note the transience of things that we previously paid very little attention to - things we habitually dismissed as having no importance, such as physical movements like bending or stretching. Any meditator who is attached to the intellect will have great difficulty in accepting the idea that wisdom can grow through such a simple and non-thinking exercise as paying attention to the transient nature of bodily sensations.

The central mental factor we need for success in meditation is mindfulness (*sati*). Like meditation itself, mindfulness is essentially a very simple thing. If we are mindful, we are aware of what is occurring in the moment; the mind is filled with what is present. Unfortunately, for many westerners the word mindfulness has connotations of thinking - which is why my teacher has suggested that sometimes a more useful translation of *sati* might be mindlessness.

Paying attention mindlessly – that is, without discursive thought – is what true mindfulness is all about. This can be a difficult point to convey, and this is in part because we tend to assume that any mental activity performed without some sort of conscious thinking is necessarily unintelligent.

So much of our cultural conditioning tells us that intelligence and intellectuality are the same thing. Our society so often equates intelligence with mental dexterity and a facility with concepts. The Buddhist definition of intelligence is quite different. Buddhism views intelligence not in terms of the ability to solve mathematical puzzles or to understand Wittgenstein, but rather as the degree to which someone is able to reduce suffering. If we are truly intelligent, then we will know how to live skilfully, minimising the distress we cause to both ourselves and others.

For some, letting go of thinking in the meditation requires courage, for they have identified themselves with that aspect of their experience. They fear that if they stop thinking, life will somehow be diminished. Through direct experience they can discover that this is not the case. Even if a meditator has begun to suspect that his reliance on thinking is unreasonable, the initial leap of faith – the abandoning of a familiar and comfortable habit – is still not easy. To abandon the known can be very challenging.

One thing that can make us less enamoured of thinking is the recognition of just how inane so much of our mental dialogue actually is. Meditation reveals that much of our thinking is little more than a fairly random collection of memories and fantasies, that a large proportion of what we might have previously assumed to be conscious deliberate thought is little more than free association.

Those who find attachment to thinking particularly stubborn and ingrained, such that it constitutes a real obstacle to mindfulness, might have to consider developing a specific counteractive strategy. For such people, actually developing their ability to think, training themselves in logic and rationality, might be the quickest route to overcoming their attachment. Those who pursue thinking systematically must come to know its limits. Then they understand through experience that thinking is not the final answer to their problems, nor can it lead to any final answer.

Sometimes attachment to intellectuality can manifest in a very different way. You see this in meditators who develop romantic ideas about traditional Buddhist societies, their attraction to the more mediaeval aspects of these cultures being based in a rejection of modern western society. Rejection of rationality and logic is just as much of an attachment and, from the meditative viewpoint, is just as unhelpful as a passionate clinging to thinking.

As always, there is a middle way between these two extremes. Thinking has its part to play in the spiritual path. While meditative attention is non-thinking, training the mind to the point where it can pay proper attention does involve a lot of thought.

Anyone taking up meditation will have some ideas, however vague, about what it is all about and what enlightenment is (and whether or not it is actually possible). It is not possible to come to the path without views about meditation and these views inevitably affect the way we meditate. It is, therefore, important that our views are accurate. If they are not, our meditation is bound to be misdirected. Thus study of the Buddha's description of the path is important, as is investigation of our experience in the light of that study.

If the meditation is going to be really effective, analysis of experience is essential. We have to try to match the theory of the teaching with meditative experience; we have to come to experiential definitions of things like mindfulness, concentration, insight. To reject or ignore the intellect is unproductive. When used appropriately, it plays an invaluable part in preparing the mind for the task of real meditation.

* * *

Any reference to the western mind or the eastern mind is obviously a generalisation. And yet there are very real differences in cultural attitudes – compare, for example, Britain with Thailand – and these differences have an important bearing on how an individual approaches the Buddha's path.

The western mind, the eastern mind – each has their particular strengths and weaknesses. Neither is better than the other.

Something we especially value in this country – some would say overvalue – is hard work, getting things done. I'm sure that the good reputation of the meditation centre in the local community owes rather more to the fact that we've done so much to renovate and maintain the buildings than to anything else. Some people wouldn't mind what we did as long as we kept the gardens looking nice.

In so many areas of life, the use of energetic striving does, of course, work. If we have enough ambition and work very hard, we can usually succeed in our goals. It may cost us an awful lot – in terms, for example, of our health – but the basic equation reads, the more energy you put into something, the more you get out of it. So, many of us come to meditation with an unquestioned belief that success is to be achieved through hard work. If the practice doesn't seem to be going that well, we tend to assume that it can be put right merely by trying harder.

Unfortunately, in the context of meditation, this approach doesn't work. It's not wrong in any moral sense – it may be perfectly sincere and well-meaning – it just cannot succeed. A meditator who believes in that almost neo-Victorian aphorism, 'No pain, no gain', will undoubtedly experience a lot of pain and certainly no gain.

It's true that, if it is to succeed, meditation requires considerable dedication. However, the amount of effort needed to pay attention in the moment is almost insignificant. Certainly, if there is no effort, the meditation just drifts into dreams and sleep. But so many westerners habitually employ a level of effort that is much too high for successful meditation.

Right meditative effort is the sort of effort that can be repeated many, many times. To many, this level of effort feels much too low; it feels as if they are just not doing enough. Such people are tempted to start doing more, to try harder. Unfortunately, this increased effort results in rising tension and a decrease in the ability to pay meditative attention.

A meditator needs to learn to employ a very light touch. Part of this process involves being patient with the meditation when it might seem too superficial. If one is patient and just carries on bringing the mind back into the moment, then the mind will gradually become more settled.

The correct use of effort in meditation is very subtle. While paying attention in the moment requires minimal effort, remembering to be mindful – remembering to return the mind, time and time again, to the observation of transience – requires much work. And we often have to use considerable effort to restrain the desire to employ more effort in the moment.

Sometimes this tendency to over-effort is exacerbated by the belief that the various factors of mind needed for meditation – such as mindfulness, concentration and even effort itself – have to be developed to an extraordinary degree.

It is more accurate to say that we already possess all the necessary factors of mind – we already use qualities like mindfulness and concentration in everyday life. For meditation these qualities do not need to be increased – rather, they need to be balanced and directed in the appropriate way. Meditation requires subtlety, not force.

★ ★ ★

The heart of the Buddha's way is the mindful observation of transience. One of the most important supports for mindfulness – and something which is of inestimable value to all meditators – is the complementary practice of *metta* or loving-kindness.

Metta meditation is an antidote to hatred. Its purpose is to develop a bias in the mind towards seeing positive qualities – in people, in situations, in anything at all. Initially, many of us display a more pronounced tendency towards fault-finding – we are already perfectly skilled in seeing the shortcomings of people. This means that, rather than paying attention to things as they are, we tend to perceive the world through a filter of negative criticism.

This negative bias in the mind is counteracted by the positive bias of *metta*. For insight practice to succeed, the resulting, more balanced outlook is essential.

Metta meditation brings tremendous benefits, and yet it can cause many westerners real problems. The main reason for this is that the practice of *metta* begins with the direction of friendly thoughts towards oneself.

Many meditators insist that they cannot do *metta* towards themselves. They have no objections to practising *metta* towards other beings, but as for themselves ... One Tibetan teacher was rather puzzled when he encountered this attitude in some western students. He commented that such low self-esteem was more appropriate to beings in the lower realms.

The practice of *metta* cannot succeed if we do not first practise it towards ourselves. How can a mind that refuses to let go of self-hatred ever hope to let go of hatred towards others? Those reluctant to develop thoughts of *metta* to themselves might like to consider just how conceited their position actually is. Would they really maintain that they have no positive qualities at all? If they concede that they have even a single positive trait, then they can use that as a starting-point for developing *metta*. Essentially, *metta* is simply a re-focusing of the mind on the positive.

★ ★ ★

In the East, many households have a copy of a Buddhist text which is kept in pride of place - up on a high shelf somewhere, occasionally dusted off and bowed to on holy days. It's rare that anyone would ever think of reading it.

It's interesting to note that the Pali Canon was translated into English quite some time before it was translated into the native languages of some of the traditional Theravadin Buddhist countries, such as Sri Lanka, Thailand and Burma.

Westerners can approach the teaching with a freshness of approach not easily achieved by those who have been steeped in Buddhist tradition since birth. One of their strengths is their readiness to question assumptions. They are not in general happy to accept something just because it is part of a spiritual tradition – they want to understand for themselves. This thirst for personal understanding is a quality essential for successful meditation.

However, the desire to question everything can be taken too far. It is essential that it is balanced with the direct understanding of the teaching that can only be gained through meditation. It's one thing to dismiss such cultural accretions as bowing to books and blessing new houses, but sometimes meditators can be too hasty. They can be too keen to reject certain practices, not realising that they are an integral part of the Buddhist way.

For example, the practice of generosity (*dana*), so strongly emphasised in the Buddhist tradition, is crucially important to someone walking the path. (The same could be said of respect for teachers and the practice of *metta*.) Many of the practices and ideas within Buddhism **are** foreign to the average westerner – that does not make them disposable. Those who have attempted to popularise the teaching and make it less foreign to modern western sensibilities have ended up simply throwing the baby out with the bath-water.

Once, the people of Thailand, Japan and Tibet regarded

the Buddha's teaching as a foreign import; centuries later it had become an integral part of their cultural heritage. A hundred years ago, Buddhism arrived in the West. Perhaps a lasting western style of Buddhism will emerge, perhaps not.

But in the final analysis, the Buddha's teaching remains alien to each one of us until we come to realise these ancient truths for ourselves. The foreign land is nowhere but in our own minds.

House of Inner Tranquillity
November 1995

It's Monday Morning -
It Must Be The Human Realm

April 1995

*The famous Thai teacher Buddhadasa said that the very
term 'human being' implies fatigue, exhaustion, shedding
sweat and hard work. He said that the essence of being
human is 'to work to get things one wants honestly and
fairly, purchasing them with the sweat of one's brow. In
short,' he continued, 'the meaning of "human being" is a
condition of habitual fatigue.'*

It's Monday Morning -
It Must Be The Human Realm

*I*n Buddhist cosmology nagas are serpent-like beings associated with water and jewels; they also have magical powers. There's an episode in the Pali Canon concerning one of these creatures who, troubled and ashamed by his birth as a naga, longed to be reborn as a human being. He eventually hit upon the idea that ordaining as a monk would be the quickest way to win human status.

One of the magical powers that nagas possess is the ability to transform their body shape and appearance at will. This naga took on the form of a young man, approached some monks and was duly ordained. Later, he came to be sharing a hut with another monk. One night this other monk was practising walking meditation and the naga-monk, confident that he was alone, fell asleep.

The Buddha later explained that there are occasions when, for all their psychic powers, nagas revert to their true bodily form. And one of these is when they completely relax in sleep.

The other monk, having finished his walking meditation, decided to return to his hut. But, opening the door, he saw, in the words of the Canon, 'the whole dwelling-place full of snake, his coils protruding through the windows'. The monk cried out in terror. Other monks came running and the commotion woke the naga. The naga confessed that he was truly a naga and explained why he had become a monk.

The matter was reported to the Buddha, who then called all the monks together. The Buddha addressed the naga, saying, 'Indeed, you nagas are not liable to growth in this teaching.' He went on to instruct the naga in how best to behave in order to win human rebirth.

It seems, though, that the naga was far from cheered. 'Thinking, "It is said that I am not liable to growth in this teaching", pained, afflicted, shedding tears, he departed, having uttered a cry of distress.'

Buddhist teachings state that there are thirty-one different realms of existence. There are the realms populated by nagas, garudas, kumbhandas, yakkhas, petas, asuras, all kinds of devas, animals and, of course, human beings. Most cultures have had similarly diverse cosmologies. Whether animistic or theistic, or perhaps more commonly a mixture of both, societies have their hierarchies of beings and spirits. Not so long ago, here in Europe, we believed in all sorts of werewolves, vampires, angels, sprites and mermaids. It's only relatively recently that the orthodoxy of western science has taken over, and now the official view is that beings without a tangible physical presence do not exist.

Of course that's only the official view – in the West many people continue to believe in ghosts, in guardian angels and in possession. And then there's the more modern version – the belief in UFOs and extraterrestrial beings. It's as if the belief in other realms just won't go away. Although officially denied, it continues in popular consciousness in films and fiction as well as in the various alternative traditions present in society.

* * *

The law of *kamma* (*karma* in Sanskrit) states that actions have results. The positive and negative actions we perform (physically and mentally) produce results which can manifest either in this lifetime or in lives to come.

Beings are born into any one of the thirty-one realms according to the actions they have performed. Selfish actions tend to lead to rebirth in one of the lower realms, unselfish actions to rebirth in a higher realm. Rebirth in any realm is impermanent. And there's no neat progression – beings can die from a heaven realm and be reborn as an animal or in a hell realm or vice versa. Being human now is no guarantee of any future state.

The human realm lies roughly midway between the heavens and hells, and human experience is a mixture of pleasure and pain. Beings are only reborn as humans because they have performed a mixture of efficient and inefficient actions. (This is bad news for anyone who believes that they should be perfect – if you were perfect you would not have taken birth as a human being.) The

Pali word for human, *manussa*, literally means those who have sharp or developed minds. It is this quality of mental development that renders human beings more capable of both highly efficient and highly inefficient actions than any of the beings in other realms.

From the spiritual viewpoint, the most significant aspect of the human realm is that it is really the only realm from which it is possible to become enlightened.

Because of this opportunity to work towards enlightenment, Buddhism makes much of just how precious a human birth actually is. The Buddha used a very graphic simile to illustrate how difficult it is for beings to return to the human realm once they are reborn in a hell state.

Imagine that someone has thrown a wooden yoke into the sea. At the bottom of the ocean lives a turtle who only comes to the surface once every hundred years. The Buddha said that the length of time it would take for that turtle to rise to the surface and by chance push his head through the yoke would be shorter than the time it takes for the being in hell to get reborn as a human.

The culture in which the Buddha taught accepted rebirth as a fact. One unfortunate result of this view was the commonly-held idea that there was all the time in the world. Many people believed that they could put off working on a spiritual path until the next lifetime round. It's easy to imagine people thinking that they'd have just one more lifetime devoted to sensuality, and then they'd think about becoming a monk or nun.

The modern western equivalent is the meditator who thinks in terms of really getting to grips with the meditation when ... when the kids have left home, when he's more financially secure, when he's retired, and so on. Of course, ideal conditions never come; if we want to, we can always find an excuse for not working.

While someone is waiting for ideal circumstances all sorts of things can happen, things like illness and death. Perhaps their teacher dies or the teaching is no longer available. Another problem with putting off commitment is that the unchecked craving and hatred performed in the interim increases ignorance. As ignorance increases, the idea of commitment fades. As ignorance increases, the chances of being reborn human diminish.

If you think that the simile of the turtle is perhaps an exaggeration, a didactic device to get people to work, consider for a moment the relative populations of the human and the animal realms.

It is estimated that the population of spiders in the UK alone exceeds fifty billion. The total world human population is under six billion. Obviously the numbers in the animal realm exceed the number of human beings by an enormous margin. A guess that there are maybe 10,000 or 100,000 animal births for every single human birth is perhaps not too unreasonable. Then there are all the beings in hell states and other lower realms. As the Buddha said, 'Rare is human birth.'

* * *

So why is it that it is only as human beings that we can become enlightened?

Imagine you're on holiday. You're staying in a hotel room which overlooks the Mediterranean. It's about half-way through your stay - you've left all your worries behind and the date for returning home is far enough away not to have yet cast its shadow. As you wake up you become aware of the warmth of the day. You can smell the sea air and through the open window you can see the tops of palm trees swaying in the gentle breeze. You feel very rested, very relaxed and you feel content.

At such times it's very difficult to indulge, for example, resentment. If the mind gets involved with inefficiency it's far more likely to be with sensuality and craving for pleasures. This is analogous to the heaven worlds. The limited range of experiences available can only condition a limited set of responses.

Let's continue with the same example of the Mediterranean holiday. Early morning in the eastern Mediterranean. Suddenly armed men burst through the door, there's a blast of automatic gunfire, your companion dies instantly, their body splattered across the walls of the room. The men grab you, beat you, tie your hands and feet and blindfold you. You're dragged out and thrown into a confined space which you quickly realise is the boot of a car. As the car speeds away you're struggling to breathe and desperately trying to remain conscious.

Again, the extreme circumstances condition a very limited set of responses. Such a hell state is far more likely to evoke terrible fear and panic rather than tranquillity or craving for some new clothes.

It's only in the human realm that we can experience the full range of both pleasure and pain, and it's only as human beings that we can come to know the limitations of all the actions it is possible to perform in response to those feelings. It's only the human realm that gives us everything, this full spectrum of experience that we need in order to become enlightened.

Materially, emotionally or spiritually, human beings can experience great richness or terrible poverty. But whatever the lifestyle, resultants are always mixed. No matter how rich people are, they still experience pain; and no matter how poor, people still experience pleasure.

All this means that the pain, disappointment and frus-.tration that we experience in the human realm is not a mistake; it's not something that we should try to avoid. Without it we wouldn't be human and could never become enlightened. Sometimes indeed it seems that the only way we ever really learn is through pain, though in actual fact it is the dynamism of pain and pleasure that is critical - consistent pain is as unproductive meditatively as is consistent pleasure.

If the human realm provides such an ideal environment for coming to the cessation of suffering, why is it the case that enlightenment is not commonplace? Just as human birth is rare amongst beings, interest in enlightenment is rare amongst humans. And of those interested in enlightenment, few ever do much about it.

Perhaps it can be said that one of the reasons human beings fail to learn is that, figuratively, they spend so little of their time being human. Human beings have the capacity and opportunity to observe and reflect on their experiences. In the hell realms beings are so caught up in dis-ease and distress that they don't have the time or psychological space for such reflection. And in the heaven worlds beings are so seduced by pleasure that there just isn't the psychological imperative to try to develop understanding.

The human realm is a microcosm of all the thirty-one realms. Someone who develops deep concentration can, for a time, live a life that has more of the quality of a *deva* existence. And, at that time, they have forfeited the opportunity to generate understanding that is inherent in human existence. Similarly, those indulging in sensuality are also choosing to try and maintain a sort of surrogate heaven world. Those who have decided that being miserable is a good credential, on the other hand, or those obsessed with resentment and envy are choosing to imitate hell beings. Whenever we move into a self-chosen heaven or hell, in a very real sense we move out of the human realm.

This doesn't of course mean that the essence of being truly human is to inhabit some bland, grey psychological area. On the moment-to-moment level, we experience the arising and passing away of feelings. This is a completely inevitable fact of life. Feelings range from the extremely painful to the extremely pleasurable - individual moments of heaven and hell if you like, and everything in between.

It could be said that to be truly human means to experience this highly dynamic procession of feelings and all other aspects of mind and body without condemning, censoring or attempting to perpetuate or destroy any one fleeting moment.

★ ★ ★

The human realm contains an enormous diversity of lifestyles and cultures. Cultural values, cultures themselves, come and go, but always there's an interplay of good and evil, efficiency and inefficiency. Because hatred and craving are an integral part of the human realm there can never be a human utopia, although the belief that there was once a golden age or that a perfect society can be created is perennially popular. For example, some have recently suggested that the growth of the Internet is 'heralding an expansion in human consciousness'. The idea may be very naive but it's hardly unexpected, given western society's difficulty in distinguishing between knowledge and wisdom.

Buddhist and Hindu cosmologies both include the idea of repeating cycles of different ages when spiritual values grow and then decay. But even during the times when the powers of either good or evil come to dominate, the opposing force is never very far away.

Even during the lifetime of the Buddha – when it's said 1,250 people became enlightened and the society of the day was happy to support an order of monks and nuns numbering many tens of thousands – corruption, warfare and torture were still commonplace. Today we live in a society that can sometimes seem terminally materialistic, and yet for the first time we have access to the teachings of all the many different schools of Buddhism – a situation that has no historic precedent.

★ ★ ★

Perhaps the main indicator of the mental health of a human society (or for that matter an individual) is the degree to which the law of *kamma* is understood. If a society ignores the fact that inefficient actions produce painful results, then there is far more likely to be wide-spread selfish action and therefore an inexorable increase in suffering. When, however, *kamma* is understood, a greater degree of happiness is guaranteed. Of course, there will always be some ignorance for, without it, beings, human or non-human, would not be reborn.

Because of this pervasive ignorance, beings often fail to see the workings of *kamma* – in other words, they make the wrong links between their actions and the results of those actions. All beings perform actions believing that, in some way, they will be of profit to them. So human beings kill, rape and steal because they believe, however fleetingly, that those actions will make things better. Of course, they don't, but people sometimes continue to ignore the true results of actions not just for years but for lifetimes, and therefore continue to act in ways that increase rather than decrease distress.

On an individual level, a child might learn that whenever it gets ill it gets more attention and affection from its parents. It decides that getting ill - or, even better, appearing to get ill - is a very good way of getting what it wants. Such a pattern of behaviour can last for decades. If necessary people produce very real, serious medical conditions just because they believe that it gets them what they want.

In fact, the real results of such self-concerned actions are exclusively painful. Such people become trapped by their web of deceit. They become much less effective in the world and, rather than lavishing affection on them, others tend to avoid them.

Those who understand the law of *kamma* know that they are totally responsible for their own lives; they know that they alone are responsible for their minds and their happiness. They know that the results of action can manifest at any time, in this or a future lifetime. Therefore, when some personal disaster strikes out of the blue - say an apparently unjustified attack on one's reputation - those with right view recognise that such an event occurs only because they have acted inefficiently in the past.

The same principle holds true with successes. For example, take a woman with an understanding of *kamma* who tries to develop concentration. She applies herself skilfully over a period of time and, when various signs associated with deepening concentration begin to arise, she recognises that this is simply the result of the hard work she's put in. She doesn't therefore indulge in elation nor does she choose to believe that her ability to concentrate marks her as an extraordinary being.

Even if an individual's belief in *kamma* is rather tenuous, the mere possibility that events are not random and meaningless enables him or her to react much less indulgently to both failures and successes.

It is a fact that, on the mundane, conventional level, we are all interdependent and interrelated in countless ways. Whenever we act in a selfish way we are attempting to create an isolated, independent existence. The more we persist with selfish action, the more we separate and estrange ourselves from reality. At such times we may find ourselves under attack, often from quite unexpected quarters.

Anyone who acts selfishly performs actions which offend others. Such a person, through their selfishness, creates situations which inevitably lead to them being badly treated by others.

I recently met someone who has convinced himself that he is a spiritually advanced being. He has chosen to believe that he is better than those around him. Such conceit is actually very difficult to maintain.

In this man's case, all his friends have got fed up with him and he suffers from frequent headaches. He is still ignoring everything life is throwing at him to make him see the error of his ways. The more he maintains his barriers, the more his problems will multiply.

If this man were to drop his conceit, his life would improve instantly. If he were to see that he actually experiences the same hatreds and cravings as those around him, his isolation would diminish dramatically. And if he started acting in a predominantly unselfish way, his life would be completely transformed.

Unselfish actions - actions which benefit and enrich the lives of others - stem from a recognition (which may or may not be conscious) of the fact that we are all inter-dependent. Such actions, based on a view that is consistent with the way things truly are, create a harmony between beings which cannot fail to smooth our journey through life.

* * *

Western society certainly doesn't score very highly for its understanding of action and results. In general, the law of *kamma* is not recognised. Instead, people genuinely believe that life isn't fair. They believe that you can act anti-socially, even criminally, and that it is possible 'to get away with it' and not to experience any unpleasant result - as long as you don't get caught, that is.

When people no longer believe that actions have results, then there is immediately much less reason to act ethically. Fear of hell states is far more of a restraining influence than is a judicial system that appears to be undecided if we are truly responsible for any criminal action we might commit.

When *kamma* is not understood, then people become very confused over the whole issue of responsibility. Indeed, people are far more likely to think in terms of their rights as opposed to their responsibilities. For example, a woman was driving along a mountain road in northern California when she noticed some climbers on a rock face on the other side of the valley. Instantly engrossed by their dangerous manoeuvres, she drove straight into a tree. Her response was to sue the climbers.

Of course, there are places where a much greater degree of right view exists. Sometimes right view crops up in the most unexpected places. The American serial killer, Jerry Dahmer, said that although it would have been very easy to blame his crimes on his parents and the way they brought him up, he realised that it had all been his own choice and that he had to live with the terrible consequences of his actions. Not the sort of response you might expect in a society where it sometimes seems that no one wants to take responsibility for anything without first taking legal advice. But the human realm always does contain all the opposites …

To someone seeking enlightenment, the views society holds are not that important. If a path to enlightenment still exists and there are teachers of that path, then enlightenment is possible irrespective of the beliefs of society at large.

To someone seeking enlightenment, the instruction of an enlightened teacher is critically important. Very few are ever going to make any significant progress without such contact, which is one of the reasons the Canon stresses the importance of respect for such teachers.

In a discourse to the Vajjians recorded in *Digha Nikaya*, the Buddha states that as long as they continue to support and protect the enlightened amongst them, then their society will continue to prosper. If a group respects such people, then it necessarily follows that it places a high value on unselfishness. Thus there is a bias towards efficient action, which is certainly the best safeguard against those destructive tendencies latent in every culture.

For the individual, however, no matter what the general level of ethical behaviour in a society, the Buddha's path to enlightenment is always 'against the stream'. In many ways, the path to enlightenment is just as difficult in a culture which respects spiritual values as in one which doesn't. The high social status enjoyed by monks and nuns in Buddhist countries has sometimes led to problems. The traditional commentaries on the teaching specifically cite fame and prestige as obstacles to meditative progress. By way of contrast, I don't think anyone in the West is likely to gain much kudos from dedication to the path to enlightenment – Buddhists become more newsworthy through political or social action.

To develop real wisdom, mundane or supramundane, we must first accept responsibility for our actions. As Alan James has said, the meditator has given up the right to ever again say, 'Look what you made me do.'

If this emphasis on responsibility makes the human realm sound like hard work, well, it is. The famous Thai teacher Buddhadasa said that the very term 'human being' implies fatigue, exhaustion, shedding sweat and hard work. He said that the essence of being human is 'to work to get things one wants honestly and fairly, purchasing them with the sweat of one's brow. In short,' he continued, 'the meaning of "human being" is a condition of habitual fatigue.'

In the traditional Theravadin ordination ceremony, a monk takes on either what is called the burden of the books (he devotes himself to study) or the burden of meditation. Contrary to what a lot of people think, recluseship is hard work, more so in some ways than having a conventional job, because for the monk or nun there is never any time off. If they are conscious, then there is always meditative work that can be done.

Trying to understand the complexities of Buddhist philosophy is a difficult thing to do; developing concentration, developing mindfulness - it's hard work. To inspire us to overcome our habitual mental laziness, the Buddha once used the following analogy.

Picture a beautiful young dancer, he told the monks, performing on the street in front of an enthusiastic audience. A man is told to pick up a bowl filled to the brim with oil and carry it around, weaving his way between the girl and the crowd. The man is followed - someone is walking right behind him with an upraised sword, poised to strike. If he spills a drop, he loses his head.

The Buddha said, 'What do you think, monks? Would that man allow his mind to wander from that bowl of oil and let himself become distracted?'

We **can** develop mindfulness but we shouldn't underestimate just what a difficult task it is. So many of our problems with the meditation arise because this is something we are reluctant to accept. So often people look for shortcuts to success (the usual one being excessive effort) or have the attitude that the meditation can somehow mysteriously take them beyond the hard work of paying attention to their unruly state of mind.

The same thing is true of other areas of human experience. Problems arise with relationships when we believe that we do not have to keep working at them. Friendships need to be looked after - taking someone for granted is a sure way to conflict. Even if we work very hard and develop *metta* (loving-kindness) so it's a real strength, if we stop exercising it then it will weaken. Any skills we have will atrophy if we do not put in the work necessary to maintain them.

As work is so central to the human realm, it seems reasonable to conclude that, in general, those who have never needed to work are not going to be able to get the full benefit of their human birth; specifically, they are not going to be able to make progress towards enlightenment.

Many religious traditions have warned against the problems of excessive wealth. The rich person can buy his or her way out of so many of the problems inherent in the human realm. Because of all his money and the power it brings, such an individual is from the spiritual view-point in the unfortunate position of being able to main-tain a view of his own independence.

For most of us, of course, work is inescapable. Even the keenest lay meditators will spend something in the region of three or four times the number of hours working than they will spend in formal seated practice. Therefore, unless work is seen as part of the spiritual path, we lose much of the opportunity presented by our human birth. People who believe that work is not part of the path also tend to see the path as not being work. But to succeed with the practice we need to have the opposite view: we have to realise that work is the path and that the path is work.

The Buddha said that work's end is man's ideal and I don't think there are many who would disagree. Very loosely speaking, we could say that there are three ways of getting to work's end.

Firstly, there is the inefficient method - get reborn in one of the lower realms. This is roughly analogous to those in the human realm who become so neurotic as to be incapable of working. This way you certainly avoid work, but the price you have to pay is very high - you merely replace having to work with something many times more unpleasant.

Secondly, we can perform efficient actions and get reborn in a heaven world. Heaven is all well and good but one day our stay there will end and heaven will be replaced by something relatively painful, coarse and demanding. It's said that just before devas die, they experience terrible suffering, knowing that their life of pleasure is coming to an end. For most people, going back to work after a fortnight's holiday is bad enough.

And thirdly, there is enlightenment. As the Canon says, at enlightenment the man or woman has dropped the burden, done what was to be done. They no longer have to work at becoming anything (such as a better meditator) or at maintaining an existing image.

But enlightenment is not inactivity. Without the instruction of the Buddha and all the other enlightened teachers right down to the present day we would not be here this evening. Enlightenment is beyond everything including activity and inactivity.

Work is *dukkha*. Enlightenment is the cessation of *dukkha*. On the one hand, at enlightenment what was to be done has been done - on the other, some enlightened teachers work incessantly to instruct others. The only way to resolve these apparently contradictory statements is through meditative experience. Then each of us can come to understand what Buddhadasa, who spent decades teaching, meant when he described enlightenment as 'all day long and nothing to do'.

The Thing Is ...

October 1993

The word dharma is now well-known in the West. Since the days of Kerouac, it has become part of the vocabulary of popular culture. But few realise that one of the meanings of dharma is 'thing'.

This talk looks at things and thingness and suggests that things aren't quite what they seem ...

The Thing Is ...

*T*he Sanskrit word *dharma*, which translates into Pali as *dhamma*, has many meanings. John Blofeld, one of the pioneering translators of Chinese Buddhist texts, commented that a word-for-word translation of a certain passage from the writings of one meditation master would run something like this: 'Dharma original dharma not dharma, not dharma dharma also dharma, now transmit not dharma dharma, dharma dharma how can be dharma.' He goes on to say that his own translation of this passage was based on the work of a certain Buddhist scholar resident in Hong Kong who was called Mr Pun.

In the Pali/English dictionary several columns are entirely devoted to the multifarious definitions of *dhamma*. Perhaps it is most commonly used to mean the Buddha's teaching, although it can denote any teaching. It can also mean duty, justice, constitution, mental object or law.

The Buddha said that *dhamma* was his banner, his standard; he said that he honoured *dhamma*. Here *dhamma* means the law of life, to which the Buddha said he was deferential and respectful.

Dhamma also means thing. What sort of things are dhammas? Basically, everything. Countries, ideas, systems of economic organisation, people, neuroses, concepts, sounds, descriptions of enlightenment.

But what exactly is a thing? How should we define a thing? This might seem a strange question because we use the word thing many times each day without it causing any problem, and yet if we try to define thing it can be quite difficult. If you ask people what a thing is, they often use the word thing in their attempts to come to a definition.

We might say that that which is discriminated is a thing.

According to Buddhism, consciousness is always consciousness of an object; if there is no object - in other words, no thing - then there can be no consciousness. The objects of consciousness are all things - as is consciousness itself. Things are the stuff of duality.

* * *

The down-to-earth, normal, conventional view of reality is that the world is made up of separate, discrete things - rocks, plants, houses, families. This view says that we know the real world exists out there through our senses, and all of us except the insane relate to the same reality made up of more or less the same things.

This contrasts dramatically with the teachings of oriental philosophy. Hinduism describes the world as being *maya*, an illusion, and *Buddhadhamma* states that the world rests on ignorance – that the world we think we live in only exists because of an error in seeing.

Speaking very broadly, the everyday view is that the world is real, made up of real things, whilst spiritual teachings such as Buddhism state that Reality (with a capital R) is beyond things – that things, truly, do not exist. An alternative translation of Blofeld's Chinese text could begin, 'The fundamental doctrine of the teaching is that there are no things.'

★ ★ ★

Conventionally, an island is a real thing. A piece of land surrounded by water. Perfectly straightforward. But if we try to rigorously define and describe an individual island various problems arise. For example, we might try to measure an island's coastline. After all, it should be possible to accurately measure something as real and solid as an island.

The mathematician Mandelbrot, one of the founders of Chaos theories, wrote a paper on just this question. He argued that, contrary to everyday expectation, any coastline can be seen as being infinitely long or, more practically, he said its length depends on the length of your ruler.

Suppose that a surveyor takes up a set of dividers, opens them to the length of one yard and walks them along the coastline. The measurement he comes up with is an approximation, because the dividers skip over twists and turns which are smaller than one yard. He then sets the dividers to a length of one foot and repeats the exercise. Because he can now take in more detail, the distance he measures is greater. The same thing happens when he resets the dividers at four inches.

Common sense would suggest that the measurements of the total length of the coastline, although they continue to get larger, would begin to converge on a particular final value, a figure that could be taken as the true length of the coastline. But Mandelbrot found that as the scale of measurement becomes smaller, the length of the coastline increases without limit. There are bays and peninsulas which reveal sub-bays and sub-peninsulas, layer upon layer, right down to the microscopic level.

Add to this the fact that levels of water around an island are variable. Tides obviously complicate measurement. Is the land that is exposed at low tide part of the island? The solid island is not quite the definite object that it is so easy to take for granted.

The definition of an island gets more complex the closer we look into it. We are used to hearing it said that no man is an island but from this point of view it begins to look as if no island is an island. Solid objects, things, have a way of dissolving and becoming more and more indefinite the more we try to define them.

Moving down in scale from islands, consider the temperature within a test-tube. A microbiologist needed to measure temperature changes caused by a biochemical reaction within a test-tube as part of a project he was working on. The problem he kept encountering was that whatever he used to try to measure these minute temperature changes, the measuring equipment itself altered the temperature.

If things and their qualities, such as islands or temperatures, were truly real, if they were truly separate, discrete and dependable, then we should be able to define and measure them accurately without running into endless problems. This difficulty is perhaps most clearly seen at the subatomic level where scientists' definitions of particles leave everyday assumptions about the world far behind. They talk about being able to know either the position of a particle or its velocity but not both, or about subatomic stuff merely having a 'tendency to exist'.

* * *

At the conventional level, you could fly to Sri Lanka this evening and know that in all probability it will still be there and that the temperature will be somewhere around 30°C. But even this conventional world, which it is so easy to take for granted, is a lot less agreed upon than most people think.

I read recently that certain Southern Baptists have calculated exactly who in the state of Alabama is 'saved' and who is not. Apparently 53.9% of the population are bound for heaven. They made these calculations by taking the numbers of church members within the population as a whole and then using certain formulae to work out the proportion of those churchgoers who were going to be saved. The closer in beliefs a church is to the Baptists, the more of its members are going to get to heaven. I'll give you one guess where, according to this Baptist belief, we are all going to go - along with all Jews, Hindus, atheists and people who like to lie in bed on Sundays.

For some the idea of eternal hell is a very real thing - others never give it a thought. What is real for one individual can be fantasy for another. We create our own worlds through the things we choose to believe in.

Conventions, descriptions of the world, vary dramatically from culture to culture. There is a huge difference, for example, between the way in which mind and matter are seen in the West and in the East.

The West tends to see physical matter as being real and mind as an epiphenomenon or spin-off from physical activity. Usually scientists equate the mind with the brain and believe that mental activity can be measured by recording electrical activity in the brain - in other words, they always tend to reduce everything to the physical.

Contrast this with the East which has produced philosophies that state 'mind is the forerunner of all things', and where you come across statements about the physical being merely 'solidified mindstuff'. This view, diametrically opposite to that of the West, sees the physical rather than the mental as the spin-off.

Within any one community there are many different conventional realities. If we go back to the idea of a flight to Sri Lanka, for some such an event contains the very real possibility of a crash and they find their fear difficult to cope with. Others don't give a thought to such possibilities. One man I knew, however, couldn't conceive of how aeroplanes manage to stay in the air. When he did fly, he exerted huge amounts of energy attempting to keep the plane airborne through the force of his will.

There are as many different views of reality as there are people. We each have our own views about what is real and all these views are quite arbitrary. We choose to believe in different things - it's no wonder that communication can be so difficult.

* * *

Sometimes the beliefs we hold are very black and white –
things are either right or wrong, true or false, real or
unreal. At other times, we operate what we might call a
sliding scale of 'realness'. This sliding scale ranges from
what we believe to be definitely real at one extreme,
down through the relatively real, then the relatively unreal
and, at the other extreme, the definitely unreal.

Let me give you some examples. Firstly, let's take the
question of astrological influence. There are people who
believe that it is undoubtedly a very real thing and some
who make it central to the way in which they lead their
lives. There are still societies, for example, which plant and
harvest crops at specific phases of the lunar cycle. A recent
American president is said to have timed various important events, such as his presidential inauguration, to coin-
cide with the most auspicious astrological influences.

Others believe that there is no such thing as astrological
influence. Several years ago a group of prominent scientists,
including Nobel prize winners, published a declaration
which appeared in the major American newspapers stating,
in effect, that astrology was nonsense. (People can and do
become very attached to the ideas they hold about reality.)

Many people's views about astrology fall between these
two extremes. Some might all but dismiss it rationally but
still find themselves interested in, and responding to, what
a magazine article on sun signs has to say. Their ambiva-
lence shows that they believe astrological influence to be
neither totally real nor totally unreal, but somewhere in
between. Sometimes we might not consciously believe
that something is real but we do emotionally, or vice versa.

Attitudes towards emotions themselves follow a similar
pattern to those about astrology. For some, their emotions
are the most important, the most real thing in their lives.

Others regard them as being insubstantial or an inconvenience or, in the case of the repressed, they no longer even see them.

Another example: a man in an office compliments a female colleague on what she's wearing. To some people that constitutes sexual harassment, to others it is no such thing. To most, perhaps, such an episode may or may not constitute harassment depending on the specific context. The individual decides how real the harassment is.

If I asked you to describe what you can see as you look towards the front of this hall, I wonder how many of you would mention the shadows. How many of you even consciously noticed the shadows? They are definitely part of the visual field and yet are not usually taken to be a significant aspect of conventional reality. They are as real visually as the objects such as the Buddha figure and the flowers, but experientially we regard them as being less real - how else could we so often overlook them?

Some might point out that thingness itself is emphasised in our culture by our western languages, which are very noun-orientated. Verb-orientated languages tend to describe things in terms of processes rather than objects. But processes are just dynamic things or groups of things - they are still separated out, discriminated bits of reality.

* * *

Buddhadhamma discriminates between conventional reality and ultimate reality, two separate and distinct realities.

Conventional reality deals with the everyday world of beings, cars, houses, etc. It also deals with other realms and the beings that populate them. It's the level of *kamma* and rebirth. It deals with ideas, concepts, philosophy, art, science and politics. At this level, you, a meditator, are listening to a lecture. Later, all things being equal, you will get into a car, drive home and sleep in a bed. This is the usual worldly description of reality.

The ultimate level of reality is concerned with what might be called the highest level of relative reality. It deals with the basic building-blocks of experience. At this level there is no you or me, there is no lecture. The terms 'you', 'me' and 'lecture' are all interpretations of experience.

Conventionally, you are looking at and listening to me. Ultimately, there is the coincidence of a visual object and the sense base of eye. The visual object is just shape and colour. Shape and colour are, at the ultimate level, real. As soon as they are interpreted, then we are no longer dealing with ultimates but with conventional reality.

'Looking at someone giving a lecture' might be an accurate description of your experience from a conventional standpoint but, ultimately speaking, there is just seeing consciousness, the object of which can only be shape and colour.

The ultimate level deals with the momentary arising of mental and physical phenomena, the conventional level deals with interpretation of that sense-data. Both these levels are addressed by the teaching. The two levels are different and do not overlap, and the meditator has to know what is appropriate to each. It's not that one is better than the other - they just deal with different aspects of experience.

The teaching of the Buddha is simply an analysis of *dukkha* (unsatisfactoriness) and the way in which it can be overcome. Thus, the whole point of the discrimination between conventional and ultimate is that it helps the meditator to understand and overcome *dukkha*.

Metta, compassion, ethics - all deal with the conventional world. All are an essential part of the path, in that they help create a mind-set that is capable of paying concentrated meditative attention. Observation of the transience of the ultimates of experience - which is the essence of *vipassana* meditation - can only succeed if order has been established within the conventional world of the meditator.

Sometimes westerners have trouble adjusting to the subtleties of the relative levels of truth and reality within the teaching. They want things to be always true or always real, an attitude that's too rigid.

Consider thinking. From the point of view of *vipassana* meditation, thinking is a mental activity, it occurs in the moment, it is a real thing, it comes and goes. But at this ultimate level, the things thought about - the contents of thinking - are not real.

A *vipassana* meditator plagued by thinking in the seated practice might systematically recollect the disadvantages of thinking to try and increase his level of attentiveness, so that he might more effectively restrain the thinking. Such a recollection deals with the conventional world; it is thinking deliberately undertaken to produce a desired effect - in this case, a reduction in thinking. Therefore, at this level, the content of thinking is real and valid.

From the ultimate standpoint, the content of thinking is just fantasy and an inappropriate object of meditation. But at the conventional level, the content of thinking can be used creatively to produce a desired meditative effect.

Not to deal with the conventional world because it's not ultimately real is to miss the point. The teaching is more concerned with the usefulness of truth than with the ultimate truthfulness of truth.

Some meditators, especially those with a strong idealistic streak, might be only too keen to accept intellectually that ultimately there are no beings. But such people are the ones for whom *metta* towards beings and the appropriate actions in respect of the conventional world are most important.

And there's no point becoming too attached to the ultimate level, because that is just the highest level of relative reality. At both the conventional level and the ultimate level, things are *anicca, dukkha* and *anatta* (impermanent, unsatisfactory and non-self). Enlightenment is beyond thingness.

★ ★ ★

The world believes that things are real; it believes that things are permanent, that they can give satisfaction and that they are capable of being owned. These views are what Buddhism describes as *vipallasa* or hallucinations of perception. What the Canon calls a *puthujjana*, a term usually translated as 'an uninstructed, untrained average person', sees no reason to doubt the solidity of things. He tends to believe that everyone sees life in essentially the same way, that there is a dependable consensus reality. On first sight that might seem innocuous enough; if everyone does it, what's the problem?

The problem is, of course, *dukkha*. If we believe that things are permanent and can bring lasting happiness, then it makes every sense to put forth great efforts to acquire and hold on to them - in other words, such a belief makes craving seem a very good idea. The things we crave for might not necessarily be inefficient - we might crave for a mind filled with *metta* - but, as the

Buddha so often stressed, craving always leads to suffering.

When we start to practise *vipassana* meditation, one of the first of the many lists we come across is that of the three marks of all conditioned things. We learn that Buddhism states that all things are impermanent and unsatisfactory, and that nothing can ever stand alone (which is, of course, the opposite of the three *vipallasa*). We hear it said that things are so impermanent, so fleeting, that they can hardly be said to exist at all.

The mark of *anatta* describes how things can only exist dependent on the presence of the appropriate conditions, how one fleeting thing can only arise due to the coincidence of many other fleeting things. So right from the start our assumptions about the things that we think make up the world are challenged. When we begin to gain experience of the three marks, then the reality of many of the things we had previously believed in is seriously undermined.

To gain real insight we have to observe things in terms of ultimates. It's possible to gain a certain amount of insight into the three marks from the conventional standpoint, but it is too superficial to seriously undermine hatred and craving. Conventionally, we can see that all things must be transient. We can observe the transience of the seasons, buildings, governments, relationships and people. We can even gain circumstantial evidence for the fact that mountains are impermanent. But such intellectual understanding doesn't really affect our emotional responses. Knowing that the mountain is transient isn't exactly going to stop us craving for a skiing holiday.

To overcome hatred and craving we have to experience the three marks at the ultimate level. We have to see that not only are our interpretations of things transient but also that the very building-blocks of our experience, the raw sense-data, are themselves utterly transient. Seeing the impermanence of moment-to-moment experience is what negates self-concern. Direct experience of the impermanence of everything that constitutes our world undermines hatred and craving. It is not possible to hate or crave for things if it is accurately seen that they are in fact dying in the moment.

★ ★ ★

The world emphasises the differences between things while the meditative path emphasises the common ground, the fact that all things are *anicca, dukkha* and *anatta.*

Whenever we grasp at things, we solidify them. Whenever we hate and crave, we emphasise the very thingness of things, we focus exclusively on those qualities that make things unique. For example, if someone craves for a new car, he or she can become so obsessed with their quest for something rare, customised or outrageously expensive that they completely forget that cars are basically a means of getting from A to B. Identification and craving can turn a simple car into a statement about who we are or who we aspire to be.

In contrast, paying attention to the three marks begins to undermine the thingness of things. Observing transience shows us that things are not the solid objects we had always imagined. If things just dissolve as we observe them, where does that leave the qualities that made those things unique, different and special?

Seeing the mark of *dukkha* emphasises the treacherous nature of things, that things are not - as we'd once assumed – dependable. And seeing the mark of *anatta* shows us that things cannot ultimately be controlled or manipulated, that they have no essence and that they can never stand alone.

But paying attention to the three marks is still dealing with the impermanence, unsatisfactoriness and non-self aspect of things. *Vipassana* attenuates thingness. Through insight things are seen to be incredibly fleeting and insubstantial but, if we are observing transience, then we are inevitably observing the transience of things.

To become enlightened we have to go beyond even the ultimates, we have to destroy the belief in separate things. Enlightenment is knowing that any division of reality into things creates a world which is *dukkha*. Because this is subtle, many have jumped (and still do jump) to the conclusion that *nibbana* is extinction. But *nibbana* is not nothing: it is beyond things, indivisible.

Nibbana is indescribable because words can only describe things. In attempting to describe the indescribable, a Chinese teacher said, 'It is without beginning, unborn and indestructible. It is not green nor yellow, and has neither form nor appearance. It does not belong to the categories of things which exist or do not exist, nor can it be thought of in terms of old and new. It is neither long nor short, big nor small, for it transcends all limits, measures, names, traces and comparisons. It is that which you see before you – begin to reason about it and you at once fall into error.'

The Shadow of the Mountain at Evening Time

October 1989

Reducing a spiritual way to merely doing good means that the world loses something of inestimable worth. The first responsibility of those who follow the Buddha's path is to become enlightened, to render themselves incapable of selfishness and harmfulness.

The Shadow of the Mountain
at Evening Time

Naropa was born a prince in Bengal round about the
beginning of the eleventh century. He left home at
a young age to study the Buddha's teaching and after
many years became very erudite, eventually being
appointed to one of the senior positions at Nalanda, the
most renowned Buddhist university in India.

In middle age, he came to realise that although he was
famous throughout the country he only knew 'the words
and not the meaning' and so set out in search of a teacher.
Eventually, after many difficulties, he encountered his
guru, Tilopa, who tested him relentlessly and severely.

At one time it was his job to supply almsfood to
Tilopa, who was living in a dense forest. One day Naropa

was out collecting food when he arrived in a town where a fair was in progress. His almsbowl was soon filled and he returned to offer the food to Tilopa.

'Naropa,' Tilopa said, 'this is delicious.'

'He seems to be in a good mood today,' Naropa thought. 'Usually he doesn't say a thing.' And so he asked him whether he should collect more food. Tilopa replied, 'Please do.' He then gave Naropa a jug full of water and a wooden sword. He said to him, 'If the people aren't willing to give, pour water on the food. If they chase after you, draw the symbol for water in the dust. And if they still do not turn back, threaten them with your sword.'

In that country it was customary to refuse alms to anyone who came to a house for a second time. People recognised Naropa and said, 'You've already had something!' So Naropa poured water on their food and ran off. Enraged, they started shouting, 'He's ruined our rice!' and they ran after him.

They were just about to catch up with him when he drew the symbol for water in the dust. A whole lake magically appeared which the pursuers could not cross. An old woman told them, 'Drain the lake.' They started digging a channel, the water ran off and soon they were able to pursue him again.

At that point Naropa waved his sword at them. It became an iron hut, inside which he found himself sitting. The same old woman said to the men, 'Get some coal and a pair of bellows. We'll set him on fire.' Overcome by the heat and fumes, Naropa could not stay inside the hut any longer. He rushed out and once more fled.

He had almost reached Tilopa when his pursuers caught up with him. They beat him senseless.

Tilopa walked over to his disciple and asked, 'What's wrong with you?' Naropa answered, 'Thrashed like rice and like sesame crushed, my head is splitting and I suffer.' To which Tilopa replied, 'This vessel of *samsara* deserves to be smashed, Naropa.'

Tonight I want to talk about *sila*, which is often translated as morality or virtue. *Sila* is the ethical framework upon which the Buddha's way rests. It is defined in great detail in the Pali Canon and elsewhere and is, on one level, quite straightforward. And yet the way *sila* is interpreted and applied makes it a highly involved and complex issue, as the story of Naropa illustrates.

The Buddha's path to enlightenment is divided into eight factors, which fall into three groups – *sila*, *samadhi* or meditation, and *panna* or wisdom. *Sila* comprises the third, fourth and fifth of the eight factors – right speech, right action and right livelihood. Traditionally, right speech is defined as speech free from lying, slander, harshness and frivolity; right action as abstaining from killing, stealing and inappropriate sexual behaviour; and right livelihood as abstaining from those livelihoods that bring harm to others, such as trading in weapons or intoxicants.

These three factors of the eightfold path are codified into the five precepts, which describe the level of ethical behaviour necessary for lay meditators to successfully follow the path. (The five precepts are rules of training to refrain from: killing or harming living creatures; stealing; sexual misconduct; harmful, deceptive and divisive speech; and indulgence in intoxicants.)

The distress occasioned by selfish behaviour was once graphically illustrated by the Buddha. He described how in moments of leisure inefficient actions return to haunt their perpetrator. 'At such times,' he said, 'those evil deeds that he has formerly wrongly done by body, speech and thought rest on him, lie on him, settle on him, as at eventide the shadows of the great mountain peaks rest, lie and settle on the earth.'

The Buddha stressed that correct *sila* was the essential foundation of the way to enlightenment. It frees the mind from guilt and remorse, rendering it calmer and more settled. But the Buddha also stressed that *sila* was not an end in itself.

On one occasion, he warned his monks about becoming content with the comfort that results from living with 'conduct in body and speech perfectly pure, clear, open, without defects, controlled'. Rather than being complacent about what they have achieved, they should strive until the true goal of recluseship – that is, the state of *nibbana* or enlightenment – is realised.

Another discourse points out that 'purity of moral habit is of purpose as far as purity of mind' – in other words, the function of *sila* is to prepare the mind for the task of developing correct meditative attention. This same discourse states quite unequivocally that 'purity of moral habit is **not** utter *nibbana* without attachment' – that is, perfect *sila* is not enlightenment. *Sila* is an indispensable component of the path but it is not itself the goal of the path.

The Buddha taught a way to enlightenment; it was not something he invented but rather something he rediscovered. He occasionally mentioned other Buddhas of earlier times, other discoverers of the way to truth, and he said that although each of them taught an effective way or *dhamma*, the length of time that their teaching survived depended on how effectively they had laid down a complementary code of ethics.

Without the appropriate rules of training, or perhaps

more commonly, when those rules are disregarded, the teaching soon dies out.

Society has definite ideas on the ways in which spiritual groups should behave. This is one of the reasons for the extreme thoroughness with which the monks' and nuns' rules were laid down by the Buddha. There are frequent references in the Pali Canon to types of behaviour which are considered inappropriate for monks and nuns because they are 'not pleasing to the manyfolk'. Things are no different today. If a group is not seen to be living up to certain standards it can expect trouble.

But if there is an over-rigid adherence to moral codes, then that also alienates people, albeit perhaps less dramatically. In this situation people recognise (perhaps only subconsciously) that the quest for truth is no longer central to the life of monks and nuns.

The Buddha described the path to enlightenment as a middle way, an avoidance of extremes. In the case of *sila*, one extreme is the total disregard of ethical conduct, the other an obsessive concern with it.

How can we tell which actions constitute this middle position? Basically, they are those actions which lead to a long-term reduction in suffering. The middle path of *sila* allows the correct development of meditation and to this end is neither too lax nor too rigid. If it is too lax there will be guilt and fear of being found out; if too rigid, there is an over-concern with rules, austerities and asceticism, and 'being good' becomes more important than being enlightened. Reducing a spiritual way to merely being good and doing good means that the world loses something of inestimable worth.

★ ★ ★

The value that society places on ethics is far from static. Looking back through history, we see an oscillation between those times when morality was regarded as all-important and the times when it was more readily dismissed. An example of this can be seen in the recent history of some Buddhist organisations in North America.

Many of these groups grew rapidly in the early 1970's, when Buddhism was still something of an exotic import, enthusiastically embraced by the burgeoning counter-culture. The more esoteric, glamorous aspects of the teaching in particular attracted much attention. Certainly there was much interest in meditation, especially when compared with earlier decades when interest in Buddhism was largely academic, but the ethical side of the teaching received little attention. Which was hardly surprising, given the then prevailing attitudes of experimentation and non-conformity.

In the '80s there were several highly-publicised scandals concerning allegations of alcoholism, abuses of power and sexual misconduct within Buddhist communities. One newsletter we received from a group in California actually suggested, somewhat melodramatically, that Buddhism in North America was dead.

Subsequent events have proved this to be far from true. But it is noticeable that the pendulum is now swinging back towards the traditionalist, conservative position. Many Buddhists are tending to distance themselves from the more innovative groups and teachers. Their journals contain articles praising traditional presentations of the teaching, monasticism and celibacy. They are also stressing the strengthening of links with established oriental schools.

So now the ethical dimension of the teaching is once again to the fore. It may become overstated to the point at which it becomes moralistic and repressive. Then the time will be ripe for a maverick figure to come along and point to the truth beyond ethics. And the cycles will repeat themselves.

One such maverick figure was Drukpa Kunley, known as the Mad Yogi of Bhutan because of the outrageous ways in which he mocked the established religious order. This is one example of his behaviour.

After he had infuriated the monks of a large monastery in Tibet with various pranks, they decided to put a stop to his mischief by burying him in a pit. To make escape impossible, the head monk even had them build a large stupa over the pit.

A few days later, the head monk was astonished to encounter Drukpa Kunley on the streets of Lhasa. 'How on earth did you get out?' he asked him.

The Mad Yogi replied that since they had done such a thorough job sealing him under the stupa, the only way he could escape had been by going down. He had gone down so far, he said, that he had reached hell. 'It was quite comfortable there,' he added, 'but rather crowded with a lot of your monks. I would have stayed there but there was only one place left, and that was reserved for you.'

* * *

In the traditional formulation of the eightfold path, each of the factors is described as 'right' (and so we have right view, right understanding, etc). Right is a translation of the Pali word *samma*, which can also be rendered in English as perfect.

In this context perfect does not mean the maximum development of the particular quality – rather it describes a level of development congruous with the development of wisdom. So perfect *sila* is that which provides the best foundation for meditation. It does not mean trying to keep the precepts 100% unbroken – which is not actually possible. Indeed the attempt to keep the precepts totally unbroken will only divert us from the real task of coming to enlightenment.

As an example, let's look at the first precept, the rule of training to refrain from killing living beings. The commentaries to the Pali Canon give clear practical guidelines which enable us to decide which actions constitute breaking this precept. They say, with typical thoroughness, that for the precept to be broken five conditions must be fulfilled: there must be a living being present; one must know that it is a being; there must be an intention to kill; there must be an effort made to kill; and, finally, death must result from the action. From this we can see that if someone accidentally treads on a snail, they have not broken the precept.

But there are times when we might decide that even conscious killing is necessary. We deliberately kill bacteria when we wash. We deliberately kill when we take antibiotics. Even the most scrupulous meditator might decide that killing woodworm in infested roof timbers is, on balance, preferable to having their roof become unsafe. Few would consider it a better course of action to let the roof collapse. And, for a meditator, the upheaval that would entail is perhaps not the most skilful use of resources and time (and there may not be as much of the latter as we'd like to think ...)

Some might say such an attitude is calculating and

hard-nosed. It **is** calculating - a meditator has to gauge the appropriateness of actions in the light of the path to enlightenment. And certainly ethical judgements do need to be completely divorced from sentimentality.

In the last analysis, as long as we are alive, we are going to kill. We destroy countless micro-organisms every time we breathe.

Buddhism, like most ethical ways, states that although killing is inefficient, killing a human being is much worse than killing an animal, which itself is worse than killing a plant. So we have an implicit scale of worth and, given the inevitability of killing, somewhere a line has to be drawn. We each have to decide whether or not it is personally acceptable for us to kill a tree that is threatening to destroy a garden wall or greenfly infesting a houseplant.

Decisions like these are not easy. When confronted with such ethical dilemmas, it's important that the meditator remembers the underlying purpose of *sila*. Essentially, he needs to establish whether or not the action in question would be detrimental to walking the spiritual path.

Killing a human being, for example, is very likely to cause insurmountable problems. Even if one is not caught and punished, the guilt and remorse may well take a lifetime if not lifetimes to subside.

The results of killing an animal are much less traumatic than those of killing a human being; while those of killing an insect are much weaker again, occasioning little in the way of mental disturbance. And the results from killing bacteria when washing begin to trail off into imperceptibility.

Knowing this, a meditator will, if necessary, be able to make the decision to spray roof timbers with woodworm killer, recognising that it is not going to be an obstacle on the path to enlightenment. He or she might well prefer not to have to kill the woodworm, but realises that not killing them would cause more problems.

The traditional wording of the precepts is 'I undertake the rule of training to refrain from ...' They are rules of training – not divine commandments – and so the odd slip here or there need not occasion guilt or self-hatred. But if they are seen as an end in themselves, instead of freeing the mind they can become yet another fetter.

For some meditators, another area of ethical concern is that of consumer spending. Some might maintain that they should boycott certain products because, they believe, their production has involved the exploitation of a workforce or the environment.

This area can become tangled and sometimes emotive. For the meditator, a clear understanding of the law of *kamma* is essential if he is going to avoid getting caught up in such issues.

Kamma means action, specifically ethical action, action that I take to achieve a desired result. The law of *kamma* states that all such actions produce results (*vipaka*). Efficient or unselfish actions produce pleasurable results; inefficient actions produce painful results. The training in *sila* ensures that the meditator no longer performs those actions which produce resultants so distressing that progress on the path is impeded.

Selfish actions, such as stealing, lying and manipulating others, are completely incongruous with treading the path to enlightenment. The path is a training in harmlessness (*ahimsa*), enlightened people being incapable of harming others or themselves.

If we personally decide to exploit other people, we

have to take the ethical consequences (which will certainly hinder our attempts to meditate). If someone else decides to exploit people, however, we cannot be held responsible for their decision. If we go into a shop and buy a pair of shoes produced by an exploited workforce, for example, we are not acting in a way that will produce resultants detrimental to coming to understanding.

The world is full of ethical dilemmas - it always has been. To resolve them all would take an infinite amount of time. Without an accurate understanding of the purpose of *sila* and its place in the path to enlightenment, it will be difficult, if not impossible, for the meditator to extricate himself from the myriad social issues that exist within human society.

A meditator must understand that *nibbana* - the total cessation of suffering - is not a political solution to the world's ills.

In laying down the five precepts, the Buddha gave those who wish to dedicate themselves to the path a guide to the limits of personal responsibility. If others choose not to live by the precepts that is their decision (value judgements have no place within Buddhist ethics). We can only ever make our own choices; we can only experience the results of our own actions.

To many westerners, this is undeniably alien. In the West we can be very quick to make moral pronouncements about the actions of others.

Some people, coming to meditation, want *sila* to be both more wide-ranging and at the same time less strict. They want Buddhism to take a moral stance on such issues as over-population and nuclear power; they don't, however, want to be told that assuming they can phone a

friend in Australia from their work place is inconsistent
with following the meditative path. To make progress on the path, we have to be impec-
cable in following the precepts. But that impeccability
does not include laying the law down for others. What
others choose to do with their lives is their own business.
But this does not mean that the meditator exists in a
vacuum. We cannot make significant progress without
developing consideration towards others. The commentaries to the Pali Canon state that a meditator can only go
so far until he has first developed those qualities known as
the *parami*. There are ten *parami* – including generosity,
metta and truthfulness – which together represent the
expression of compassion. If a meditator is not prepared to
develop compassion, enlightenment is not possible.

★ ★ ★

Buddhism lists ten ways in which we ignore reality, ten
fetters that have to be overcome before enlightenment is
possible. One of the coarsest fetters is usually translated
as attachment to rule and ritual but an alternative
rendering is misapprehension of morality and duty. Misunderstanding *sila* and having wrong ideas about where
our responsibilities really lie mean that we will continue
to be chained to the wheel of birth and death.

There is a story in the writings of the Taoist philoso-
pher, Chuang Tzu, which shows that this is nothing new.

There was a Taoist student who wished to go and live
in a particularly lawless and corrupt region, to see if he
could bring about some improvement in the conditions
there.

The master told the student that he really didn't know

what he was doing. He said, 'You will bring disaster upon yourself. Tao has no need of your eagerness and you will only waste your energy in your misguided efforts.' He went on to explain that by squandering his energy, the student would just become anxious and confused and in no fit state to help anybody, not even himself.

'If you do not have Tao yourself, what business have you spending your time in vain efforts to bring corrupt politicians into the right path?'

This misapprehension of morality and duty indicates a confusion about the meaning of the spiritual path. The person who is over-concerned with such issues as the ethics of consumer spending is hoping to establish what he sees as a fairer society, not striving to come to understanding.

The goal of the spiritual path is not a material utopia. The path is not ultimately concerned with trying to adjust mundane conditions - it aims at the transcendence of all opposites. Again, to quote from Chuang Tzu, 'He who wants to have right without wrong, order without disorder, does not understand the principles of heaven and earth. He does not know how things hang together.'

If an individual student has an attachment to rules or morality, then the teacher may resort to what might seem to be quite outrageous steps to overcome it. Which takes us back to the story of Naropa. Naropa was a prince, a famous scholar and a renowned monk. To overcome his pride and attachments, Tilopa incited Naropa to damage others' property, to assault people, to break his vow of celibacy - in fact, to break just about every rule in the book.

Similar stories exist in the Zen tradition. They aim at undermining attachment to *sila* by pointing to the fact that enlightenment is beyond both good and evil. Unfortunately, such stories sometimes get picked up by those whose *sila* is underdeveloped rather than overdeveloped. Such people can then decide that keeping rules is for lesser beings and, through their resulting unethical behaviour, they forfeit any chance of meditative progress.

So *sila* is the essential foundation of the path but its purpose and limits need to be clearly understood. Without *sila* enlightenment is impossible but *sila* cannot of itself lead to enlightenment. Perfect *sila* is the middle way between indulgence and over-rigidity.

People generally understand the pitfalls of indulgence and breaking precepts but are less aware of the dangers of going overboard with rules and ascetic practices. Someone once asked the Indian teacher Sri Nisargadatta whether austerities and penances were of any use. He said, 'To meet all the vicissitudes of life is penance enough. You need not invent trouble. To meet cheerfully whatever life brings is all the austerity you need.'

Dukkha

May 1994

This talk was given on the occasion of Wesak (the full moon of May, the day on which - according to tradition - the Buddha was born, became enlightened and died).

Dukkha is a Pali word, most frequently translated as suffering. The Buddha said, 'I teach only one thing - dukkha and how to overcome it.'

Dukkha

*I*n the last few weeks ...

Up to half a million people, it's thought, have been slaughtered in Rwanda.

The death toll and the number of refugees continue to rise in the largely forgotten war between Armenia and Azerbaijan.

Britain and the US have both lost respected public figures in John Smith and Jackie Kennedy Onassis, one to a heart attack, the other to cancer.

A young boy accidentally shot and killed his brother in the celebrations to mark the end of the Israeli occupation of the Gaza strip.

A woman in her seventies has discovered that she's considered too old to qualify for certain National Health treatments.

A meditator has been manipulated by her domineering spouse into cancelling a retreat.

An eight-year-old boy, forbidden to keep a pet, has been wondering if he might be allowed to keep a snail in a jamjar.

And the *abutilon* at the meditation centre, which has been flowering profusely since early April, looks as if it will be past its best by the time of our Open Day.

The list could go on forever. As the Buddha said, 'There is suffering.'

★ ★ ★

For Wesak it seems appropriate to go right back to this, the very heart of the Buddha's teaching. Although the *dhamma* is a huge subject and the recorded teachings of the Buddha extend to something like thirty volumes, it can all be reduced to the four noble truths. Every discourse, every list (and there are literally hundreds of those), is an analysis, an exposition, of one or more of these four truths - the truth of suffering, the truth of the arising of suffering, the truth of the cessation of suffering, and the truth of the way to the cessation of suffering.

Suffering is a translation of the Pali word *dukkha*. *Dukkha* does not translate very easily into English. The Buddha said that all things are *dukkha*, from the most intense pain to the most rarefied pleasure; in the last analysis all things are *dukkha* because they are impermanent and therefore can never bring lasting happiness. Perhaps unsatisfactoriness is a more accurate translation but I think that there is a danger that unsatisfactoriness sounds too watered down, too sanitised. It might suggest that *dukkha* is an inconvenience rather than the central problem of existence.

Some translators use the term unsatisfactoriness to avoid that frequently heard criticism that Buddhism sees all life as suffering and therefore as miserable. The Buddha never denied the pleasures that life contains - he just pointed out that they are as fleeting and unreliable as anything else and are not the true happiness we seek.

There is a list the Buddha used to illustrate the first noble truth. He said, 'The noble truth of *dukkha* is this: Birth is suffering, ageing is suffering, sickness is suffering, death is suffering; sorrow, lamentation, pain, grief and despair are suffering; to be conjoined with things we dislike, to be separated from things we like - that also is suffering; not to get what one wants is suffering - in brief, the five groups of grasping are suffering.'

These things are not just inconveniences - they are *dukkha*, suffering. We perpetuate suffering by ignorance, including ignorance of suffering itself. According to Buddhism, ignorance is a volitional activity. We choose to ignore, although it is a choice of which we may not be conscious.

If we regard *dukkha* merely as unsatisfactoriness and see it as a philosophical problem rather than a gut-level experience of pain and separation, we have already begun to ignore it. And while we ignore *dukkha* we are sowing the seeds for more suffering in the future.

Ignorance can involve more than just turning the mind away from something and acting as if it does not exist. On a more subtle level, we can ignore things by seeing them in a distorted way; we might acknowledge that something is present but refuse to recognise its true nature.

For example, a meditator in a bad mood might claim to be fully aware of that emotional state, but he or she can only perpetuate their mood by ignoring just how distressing it actually is.

As another example, I remember a meditator on retreat who had been struggling for months with the problem of falling asleep in the meditation. One day she came in moaning that the meditation was filled with endless thinking. She didn't even mention that she had stopped falling asleep. She knew that she had stopped but she dismissed it, because the practice still wasn't going the way she wanted. She had chosen to overlook the fact that the mind was no longer obsessed with sleepiness. Instead she focused on the fact that still she wasn't getting her own way.

Seeing things from this ignorant perspective, she believed nothing had really changed. She had paid no attention to the transience of things, which is what *vipassana* meditation is all about, and had thus strengthened her view of permanence.

Birth is suffering. There are those to whom such a statement is anathema, but the Buddha always said his teaching was against the stream. It's easy to take for granted western standards of health care (perhaps increasingly less so in this country) but in most parts of the world infant mortality rates are high. Many women die in childbirth and a baby can mean just another mouth to feed when food is already short. Then the baby might be the wrong sex ... In many countries female infanticide is common.

Even if health care is available and the baby is born into riches, how many babies are actually wanted? How many children are an inconvenience to their mother's career? And is not birth the beginning of one of our most difficult relationships - that with our parents? Even if the relationship is good, either you are going to witness your child's death or your child is going to witness your death.

And yet still we see birth as a happy event.

Some believe that people can carry around psychological scars throughout adulthood as a result of a traumatic birth. Given the way most people resist even a little change it's no wonder that birth is traumatic.

In the last analysis, birth is the prelude, the gateway, to all the suffering we will ever experience.

But *dukkha* is not just the life sentence - it is also the key to freedom. It is only the experience of *dukkha* that drives us to seek a way beyond suffering. Whilst we are ignoring suffering, we don't have to do anything about trying to understand it. The spiritual path entails reversing all ignorance of suffering. We have to learn to pay exquisite attention to things - including disappointment, frustration, boredom, pain, sorrow. The way to freedom is to gain a total understanding of suffering.

Another way in which we can ignore *dukkha* is by believing that it can be avoided, by believing that *dukkha* - rather than being a fact of life - is an aberration. If we believe that suffering is an aberration, we believe that it need not be there and so, naturally, we try to avoid it.

But trying to avoid suffering - which is another way of saying craving for satisfactoriness - inevitably leads to more ignorance. Whenever we crave, we abandon the moment and what is really occurring and we move into a fantasy world. Ignorance of reality always leads to suffering. Craving conditions more ignorance and ignorance conditions more craving - the original vicious circle. Craving and ignorance are the foundations upon which all suffering depends.

Craving is the belief that happiness can be found by manipulating life into giving us what we want. For example, a very successful woman in her mid-forties has decided that it's time to have her first child. Everything is planned - the timing of the pregnancy to fit around her work schedules, the in-vitro fertilisation and hi-tech medical care, the employment of a nanny and extra domestic help. Given that she is such a controlling type, she has probably already made plans for the child's education. One suspects that the being waiting to be born is not going to be completely satisfied with being little more than a designer accessory to its parents' lifestyle. We cannot use control to create a life without *dukkha,* no matter how hard we might try.

Ageing is suffering. I saw a cartoon which showed a no longer young new age traveller wearing a badge that had originally said, 'Never trust anyone over 30'. The number 30 had been crossed out and replaced with 35, which had in its turn been crossed out and replaced with 40, then 45, then 50. Ageing can seriously challenge our self-image.

Anything we might base our self-image on is transient, whether looks, riches, skills or youth. When conditions change, our self-image too has to change, unless we want to become a caricature, like the 50-year-old hippy. Having to update a self-image is *dukkha* and most people don't like to face up to the fact of ageing. I suspect that the percentage of people over the age of 35 who actually believe that policemen really are getting younger is quite high.

Bodies age, they no longer do what they used to, and they start doing things they never did before. As they say, bits get lower, wider and hairier. Some just try to ignore ageing. There are 70-year-olds who still describe themselves as middle-aged; people lie about their age, or try to dress in a style better suited to someone a couple of decades younger. Some think that they can counteract ageing with more exercise, a better diet, more cosmetics, more or different hormones, transplanting hair or other surgical adjustments.

Sometimes people ignore the psychological aspects of ageing rather than the physical - typically those who always seek to avoid responsibility.

Generally, we do slowly learn as we get older. The only problem, someone once commented, is that by the time we have learned enough to know how to live properly, it is time to die.

Scientists talk about the possibility of being able to reverse ageing chemically. It may be possible to preserve cell structure for longer periods of time, but ageing and decay are inherent, not pathological. This actually seems a good metaphor for our attitude to *dukkha* itself.

As I've said, we like to believe that suffering - like ageing - is avoidable, that we personally can outwit *dukkha* and carve for ourselves a niche in the world that is free from suffering. This view is the basis for what the Buddha called *samsara*, the wheel of birth, death and suffering. To go beyond suffering, we have to go beyond worldly conditions - we cannot find real happiness by manipulating and controlling things that are inherently flawed.

Of course, it's not just bodies that age and decay. Nation states age and decay. Recently, for example,

Jugoslavia and Czechoslovakia have ceased to exist. Maps become outdated very quickly. Empires come and go. Fifty years ago, atlases showed a large part of the world shaded red, marking the British Empire; now Britain is just a poor, rather insignificant country on the periphery of Europe.

The planet itself is ageing and decaying. With or without human interference it will one day cease to exist. And this very *dhamma* is ageing and will one day be lost. The Buddha himself described the way the teaching would gradually decay and which parts of it would be discarded first.

Sickness is suffering. Sickness is another fact of life and yet it's something else that people can see as an aberration. Some people believe that medicine, in whatever form, can make everything all right. The perfect health myth is surprisingly common. An especially pernicious form of this is that which sees ill-health as a sign that someone is doing something wrong. It's rare that anyone goes for more than a year without some sort of illness. Bodies are vulnerable things; stress causes problems, and stress can never be avoided totally.

I once came across a rather bizarre example of the view that sickness and death are not really suffering. A 'healer', talking about one of her deceased clients, said (with the sincerity in her voice turned up to maximum) that 'death can sometimes be a part of the healing process'.

Death is suffering. Unlike birth, we can't really pretend that death is a happy event, so to avoid facing up to this particular aspect of *dukkha*, we prefer to pretend that it just won't happen. The *Mahabharata* says that the greatest wonder in all the world is that people continue to believe that 'death can never happen to me today'.

In this society we hide death away; we rarely talk about it, we rarely see a dead body. We talk about death in euphemisms - people pass away, pets are put to sleep, wild animals culled, and we refer to 'the late so-and-so' instead of 'the dead so-and-so'. A hairdresser who emigrated to Canada found he could earn more tidying up the hair of corpses in funeral parlours than he could by working on the living. If we do see death, let's make sure it is as manicured as possible.

Obviously, it takes more than a few cosmetic adjustments to help us cope with death, and so most retreat back into the view that death is something that will happen to everyone else. It is not uncommon that people include in their wills an instruction to the undertaker that their wrists should be cut before the coffin lid is screwed down. It's as if they believe that somehow their own death will be some sort of mistake.

These days we see another manifestation of our rather estranged relationship with death. When a terrorist bomb explodes or the victims of a serial killer are discovered, 'carers' appear in order to give counselling to those whose lives are affected. Society now seems to believe that the provision of such counselling is normal and necessary. The emotional message is that death is aberrant, that it shouldn't happen.

No amount of counselling can take death away or remove its finality.

Because of our ingrained tendency to ignore death, and because of the complacency that that brings, *Buddhadhamma* contains formal recollections of death.

Death is suffering; as the commentaries say, it is like a

murderer with a raised sword, ready to strike at any moment. Death is the ruin of all success; it interrupts pleasure, ends relationships. Death also interrupts the spiritual path. Even though someone working sincerely and systematically at the spiritual path is creating the conditions which ensure they will gravitate towards the teaching in future lives, there is no guarantee when that will be, or whether they will again encounter such beneficial conditions under which to practise.

Sorrow, lamentation, pain, grief and despair are suffering. You might think this sounds too obvious and yet even this area of *dukkha* is ignored. One method of ignorance is to mentally override such things and repress the feelings they generate. Another form of ignorance is to do exactly the opposite and indulge in such feelings.

That might sound strange but anyone who, for example, consistently wallows in depression is ignoring *dukkha*. Or anyone who pays a therapist for years on end to listen to them retelling the same old problems - which they are not really prepared to do anything about - is also ignoring *dukkha*.

Such people might say they do accept suffering. But if they truly did, then they could never cling to sorrow, lamentation and pain and turn them into credentials. If we rightly see that something is really painful, then nothing will possess us to grasp hold of it, let alone use it to bolster our self-image. Anyone who knows that excrement stinks doesn't fill a swimming pool with it and dive in.

To be conjoined with things we dislike, to be separated from things we like - that also is suffering. The way of the world is to believe that if we can successfully control the things we experience, we can control happiness. But the Buddha pointed out that all things are *anatta,* which means that they are ultimately uncontrollable. It is completely inevitable that we shall have contact with things we find unpleasant and that we shall, at times, be separated from the things we like. It is part of our human heritage that we will experience both painful and pleasurable resultants.

And yet we persist in trying to manipulate life so that pleasure is always available. We crave for and cling to pleasurable feelings and hate painful feelings. And we ignore the fact that craving and clinging do not produce lasting happiness.

No matter how much money someone has amassed, or how much insurance he's got, or how many drugs he may take, he cannot avoid pain.

One way in which we ignore the inevitability of pain is to blame the external conditions that we believe create our distress. Beliefs that all our problems are caused by the government, or immigrants, or men, are all based on the naive view that we can avoid being 'conjoined with things we dislike, separated from things we like'. No amount of manipulation of our external conditions can ever bring lasting happiness.

The world contains grief, sorrow and pain. Human beings can act wisely and compassionately, but they are equally capable of callousness and cruelty. Hatred and craving in the environment - evil, if you like - is a fact of life which we cannot avoid.

After the James Bulger murder, many expressed the view that the child murderers were 'freaks of nature', in their attempt to explain away such an evil act. From the meditative viewpoint, extreme acts of cruelty are the outcome of unchecked hatred and craving. There is no evil apart from ignorance, craving and hatred.

Every meditator knows that evil does not just exist out there. How many of us have never experienced a cruel or murderous thought? If cruel thoughts are made much of, there will come a moment when they lead to physical action. Someone 'gets pushed too far', they lose self-control ... Is evil really that remote from us?

Through insight it is possible to destroy the roots of hatred and craving, the roots of evil. However, the possibility of falling back into grossly inefficient actions is not completely removed until a considerable amount of meditative work has been done.

There is a point on the path known as stream-winning, where the meditator has a first glimpse of *nibbana*. At this point, it is said, rebirth in a state lower than human is no longer possible and the meditator knows that final enlightenment is assured. A Burmese teacher pointed out that until beings had reached stream-winning, their natural home was hell.

Not to get what one wants - that also is suffering. Could there ever be a more pertinent or succinct description of the lot of humankind? We've talked about *dukkha* in the form of birth, ageing, sickness, death, sorrow, lamentation and woe, association with the unloved, separation from the loved, and now, with not getting what we want, the list becomes even more comprehensive. We could go on forever - having to work is suffering, feeling trapped by a sense of duty is suffering, hearing things we don't want to hear is suffering.

Not to get what one wants - that is suffering. With this statement we get an intimation of the second and third noble truths. The Buddha's teaching could be described as holographic. To analyse any one section of the teaching in full, you inevitably have to bring in the rest of the *dhamma*. Stating that not getting what we want is suffering points to the fact that it is the very wanting, the craving, that leads to suffering, and that without the craving suffering ceases.

Dukkha is the first noble truth because it is the starting-point. It is what drives us to find a way out, to seek freedom. As long as we ignore the true state of affairs we just continue around the wheel of birth and death, seeking satisfaction in the world. The perception of *dukkha* increases our desire to escape from it. Following a true spiritual path our perception of *dukkha* deepens, which in turn increases our desire for enlightenment.

In short, the five groups of grasping are suffering. We've looked at suffering in relatively coarse terms, in terms of birth and death, through to the more subtle unsatisfactoriness of not getting what we want. The list now extends the definition of *dukkha* to its limit.

The Buddha analysed all experience into five 'groups of grasping' (*khandha* in Pali). Everything we experience can be classified under the headings of materiality, feeling, perception, habitual tendency or consciousness. And every aspect of each of these groups is transient.

In saying that these five groups are suffering, everything in our experience can be classified as *dukkha*. Not just the things we don't like or the things we want but don't get, but also the things we like, the success and happiness that we do get.

★ ★ ★

The first part of the spiritual path concerns the development of *sila* or ethics. Adopting an ethical lifestyle and renouncing selfish forms of physical and verbal behaviour immediately and dramatically reduces suffering. Developing meditation, increasing mindfulness and concentration, learning to overcome such hindrances as worry and irritability, brings about another huge reduction in suffering. Gaining insight, with the consequent decrease in attachment, reduces it even further.

But it's not the case that the spiritual path gradually reduces suffering to the point where it is so attenuated it fades into nothing and that is enlightenment. The path does reduce suffering, but at the same time it deepens our understanding of *dukkha* and shows how all-pervasive it is.

The reduction in suffering brought about by keeping precepts, developing mindfulness, etc, is rightly seen as a great improvement. But it is not the final answer. The meditator knows that all things are impermanent - calm, bliss, even insight. Impermanence can no longer be ignored. The meditator sees that even the most refined pleasure, even the most fulfilling state of which he can conceive, is impermanent and therefore unsatisfactory.

The skilled meditator may have left behind the *dukkha* of such things as guilt, doubt, self-consciousness and meditative over-effort, but that is counterbalanced by his increasing awareness of the *dukkha* inherent in dualistic consciousness.

The Canon says that the experienced meditator comes to feel disgust for body, disgust for feelings, disgust for perceptions, disgust for the habitual tendencies and disgust for consciousness. Every last aspect of experience is seen as totally impermanent, treacherous, uncontrollable, utterly unsatisfactory. Feeling disgust the meditator is repelled. Being repelled, he no longer grasps at duality but turns to the unconditioned, to *nibbana*.

This is enlightenment, the destruction of the wheel of birth and death, the end of the spiritual path, the transcendence of all ideas of myself as separate from the world. It is the end of all suffering.

The Buddha said, 'I teach only one thing – suffering and the cessation of suffering.' The way to the cessation of suffering is a total understanding of *dukkha*, how it arises and how it ceases. This is gained by following the eightfold path, a path, which according to tradition, the Buddha rediscovered on this full moon of May, 2538 years ago.

The Vinaya

April 1991

*The monks had been given more food than they needed.
The Buddha told his attendant Ananda to distribute it
among other recluses - that is, to those belonging to different
monastic orders. Ananda gave some small cakes to a group of
female wanderers, handing one cake to each woman. He
hadn't noticed that two of the cakes had stuck together and
so one female wanderer ended up with two. Her friends saw
this and rounded on her, saying, 'That recluse is your lover.'*

*This lecture is about the Vinaya, the code of discipline laid
down by the Buddha for the orders of monks and nuns. It
ends with a brief look at rules in the context of a modern
Buddhist order in the West.*

The Vinaya
or Sex, Lies & Robe Material

*F*rom the earliest days, thanks to the generosity of the
lay community, the Buddha's order of monks was
extremely well-supported.

There's an account in the Pali Canon concerning an
occasion when the Buddha was touring the Ganges valley
accompanied by a large group of monks. Such was the
devotion of the lay people that many followed the monks
in wagons loaded with foodstuffs, waiting for an opportunity to prepare a meal. One of these people, it's said, had
been following the monks for over two months and his
turn to donate a meal had still not come round.

A large number of recluses and such a volume of gifts
obviously needed careful organisation and different

procedures evolved for dealing with the logistic problems
that arose.

The monk Dabba, who was said to have become
enlightened at the age of seven, decided that he could best
serve the order by organising the allocation of lodgings and
food, a decision of which the Buddha himself approved.

Dabba lodged all the chanting monks in one place
and all the meditating monks somewhere else so that
they would not be disturbed. For the sake of harmony
he also lodged all the teaching monks together and all
the talkative monks together.

Dabba also possessed a psychic power which came in
useful when monks arrived in the night. He had developed the skill of producing light from his finger. So at
night he held up a finger and illuminated the way. Some
monks were so intrigued by this that they purposely asked
for lodgings in remote places so that they could observe
the phenomenon.

At one time there were some newly ordained monks
who were acting in a very undisciplined way; because of
this, they received poor quality almsfood. When the elder
monks were given special delicacies, they used to look on
enviously while the elders ate.

One householder had issued a general invitation to the
monks, saying that each day he would feed four of their
number. Everyone knew that at this house they would
receive high quality food, beautifully served. One day
Dabba let the undisciplined monks know that the next
day it would be their turn to receive a meal at this house.

But that evening the householder visited the monastery
and happened to fall into conversation with Dabba. He
was not very pleased when he found out which monks
were to be his guests on the following day. When he

returned home, he gave instructions that they were to be served broken rice and sour gruel.

The monks were very excited at the thought of their meal. The Vinaya says that they didn't sleep much that night. But then they saw the broken rice and gruel ...

When they remembered that the householder had been to the monastery and had spoken to Dabba, they concluded that it must have been Dabba who had set the householder against them.

They plotted revenge. First they got a nun called Mettiya to go to the Buddha and accuse Dabba of assaulting her. This accusation was soon found to be groundless and as a result the Buddha expelled the nun.

The monks tried again. This time they were more cunning. While they were out walking they saw two goats copulating. One of them said, 'Let's call the he-goat Dabba and the female goat Mettiya.'

When they got back to the monastery, they told the other monks that previously they had only heard the rumours about Dabba and Mettiya – now they had seen what went on for themselves.

After an enquiry, the truth of the situation was revealed and rules about defaming fellow monks with accusations of major offences were established.

This episode comes from the *Vinaya-Pitaka* or 'The Book of the Discipline'. The Vinaya is considerably more, however, than just a list of rules.

In English translation the Vinaya comprises six large volumes, forming about a quarter of all the Canonical material. As well as containing an enormous wealth of information on the rules themselves and the penalties incurred for breaking them, it also gives the context for how each rule came to be laid down by the Buddha. In so doing, it provides a detailed picture of the everyday life of the monks and the society of the time. Thus it's of interest on many levels - historically, anthropologically, psychologically. And apart from that there's lots of sex, violence and weirdness.

* * *

One common misconception about the life and times of the Buddha is that it was a golden age in which all the monks and nuns were perfectly behaved, all either enlightened or on the brink of it.

It's true that at that time there were many very gifted people both inside and outside the order. Many of them were enlightened or at least well-established on the path; many more were committed to the teaching and dedicated to coming to understanding. Reading the Vinaya, however, very quickly reveals that there were many monks and nuns who did not fall into any of these categories.

From the early days of the Buddha's teaching career, the order of monks grew very quickly. It soon attracted royal patronage and many wealthy supporters. But this success brought its own problems. As the Buddha said, many of the conditions for the arising of corruption only come about when the order expands and acquires fame and property.

An illustration: at one time, all sorts of diseases were rampant in Magadha. In search of a cure, one man approached Jivaka Komarabhacca, the foremost doctor in the land, who attended both the royal family and the order of monks led by the Buddha. Jivaka said that he was unable to help him. He explained that he could not take on any extra patients, though the man offered him all his wealth and even promised to become his slave. The only way he could receive medical attention, the man realised, was to ordain as a monk. This he did. As soon as he recovered, he left the order. When news of this case came to his attention, the Buddha introduced a rule that monks should not ordain anyone who was sick.

Because the order was so generously supported, the monks and nuns were often well fed, even in times when food was scarce. One group of monks, when on almsround, took to covering any curries or condiments in their bowls with rice. They reasoned that if people assumed that they'd only been given rice, they would be more likely to put interesting food into the bowls.

So some people ordained for the sake of their stomachs. Others did it for what they considered to be an easy life. Still others ordained to gain status. For them, becoming a monk or nun was a way of acquiring the respect and recognition that eluded them in lay life.

When people entered the order for the wrong reasons – such as fame, food or medical care – there was bound to be trouble.

So as time went on more and more rules became necessary. The original few monks just needed some gentle guidelines. Some of the later intake needed a whole host of rules – rules about how to dress appropriately, how to relate to seniors and lay people, even rules about eating properly.

The rules were not laid down all at once – the Buddha formulated new ones as the situation demanded, as illustrated in the opening story. Thus the Vinaya evolved organically over the decades of the Buddha's teaching.

★ ★ ★

The books of the Vinaya deal with offences and rules in order of seriousness. The first category of offence is called *parajika* in Pali, which literally means defeat. A monk or nun committing such an offence is one who is defeated – that is, one who is expelled from the order for life. For monks, there are four such offences – killing a human being, stealing, having sexual intercourse and falsely claiming to have achieved various exalted meditative states.

Each of these four offences is described in great detail and the exact conditions which constitute such an offence are precisely documented.

Originally, the wording of the first *parajika* stated that 'any monk who should intentionally deprive a human being of life is one who is defeated'.

A certain group of six monks became infatuated with a lay woman, described by the Vinaya as 'beautiful, comely and pleasant'. The husband of this woman happened to be far from well. The six monks reasoned that they stood more chance with the woman if her husband died. And so they told him what a good life he had lived, and how death would be far better because he was sure to be reborn in the heaven worlds experiencing '*deva*-like qualities of sensual pleasures'. He believed them, stopped looking after himself and died.

The Buddha had to amend the original rule. He said that a monk who 'should deliberately and purposefully praise the beauty of death, or should incite anyone to death, is also one who is defeated'.

The rule was later expanded further. Should a monk command another monk to kill someone and the murder takes place, then both are defeated. But if a monk commands another monk to kill and the murder does not take place, then the first monk is only guilty of a lesser offence. Many other permutations followed.

The second *parajika* states that any monk who steals is also 'one who is defeated'. Again there is lots of legal detail but, basically, a monk deliberately taking anything he knows does not belong to him is expelled from the order.

The next *parajika* deals with sexual intercourse. A monk who has intercourse with a woman or a man, a eunuch or an hermaphrodite, human or non-human, is expelled from the order for life.

The chapter in the Vinaya dealing with this rule is frequently punctuated with asterisks, which indicate that the translator has either glossed over certain paragraphs or has left them untranslated. She writes of some passages, 'Because of the outspokenness and crudeness which they contain, and which seem to be inseparable from early literatures, they appear unsuitable for incorporation in a translation designed principally for western readers.' So I'm afraid many of the stories are unsuitable for us.

At this point it does need to be stressed that the monks' and nuns' rules are intended for monks and nuns. As an ethical guideline for lay meditators, the Buddha laid down the five precepts. As a code of conduct they are not inferior to the recluses' rules, but rather are appropriate to the very different lifestyle of the lay person. A lay man who tries to follow the monks' rules is quite misguided – just as is a monk who tries to live like a lay person.

Examples of this type of misunderstanding are sometimes found in the area of sexual behaviour. The precept states that unlawful, adulterous or promiscuous sexual activity is inappropriate for anyone following the Buddha's teaching. For a monk or nun, however, any sexual activity is inappropriate. Someone who is confused about this issue might reason that because monks and nuns are barred from sex, then sex is somehow wrong for lay people too.

Monks and nuns have renounced the world to devote all of their time to coming to understanding, and they are totally reliant on the generosity of lay supporters for their material needs. If a recluse had a sexual relationship, it's undoubtedly the case that very few lay people would be prepared to support him. And without support the order collapses. Further, such a relationship would inevitably take time away from meditation.

Sex is not incongruous with the spiritual life but it is incongruous with the life of the monk or nun. Meditators who give up sex, thinking it impure, unholy or whatever, are falling into the wrong view that sees sensory experience itself as the problem, rather than the craving for such experience. Such a view is a serious obstacle to meditation.

The fourth *parajika* offence is that of falsely claiming meditative attainments. It might seem that this offence is less serious than those dealing with killing, stealing or sexual intercourse and therefore, perhaps, shouldn't merit expulsion from the order. And yet further reflection reveals just how grave an offence this is.

Everyone wants enlightenment. They might not call it that, but everyone seeks an end to distress. If someone falsely claims enlightenment, he devalues it. In doing so, he devalues the highest goal mankind can aspire to. If other people believe that person's false claims, they are led astray; their conception of the highest is tainted. The Buddha said that someone who claimed states in this way was the greatest thief in all the worlds and that such a person would be reborn in a hell state.

After the four *parajika*, the next most serious class of offence is called *sanghadisesa*. There are thirteen offences in this category. They include such things as touching a member of the opposite sex with lust in the mind and hinting for gifts. In one episode in the Vinaya, some monks dropped so many hints about all the things they wanted that the villagers ran away every time they saw the monks coming.

These offences are not serious enough to merit expulsion from the order for life, but any monk committing one of them has to confess his error in front of the entire monastic community. In addition, he may be punished by, for example, losing various privileges or being expelled from the order temporarily.

★ ★ ★

When the Buddha founded the order of monks, he set it up in such a way that the monks were totally dependent on the laity for support. Monks were not allowed to handle money, work in employment or farm the land. Food was collected on a daily almsround and there were rules restricting the storing up of material goods. These conditions were congruous with the prevailing culture of India at that time, where there was already a long tradition of wandering recluses who had renounced the world.

Such direct dependence on the lay people had a radical effect on how the order and its discipline developed. The almsround meant that the monks were very visible in the society. Being so visible, the monks not only had to behave in a way that was appropriate to their meditative endeavours but also in a way that was culturally acceptable. Put simply, if monks behaved badly they were not fed.

The almsround created a dynamic symbiosis where the lay people gave their material support and the monks gave through teaching and example. It also created an immediate safeguard for the order: if rules were not kept and seen to be kept, then support dried up and the monastic lifestyle would no longer be possible.

This is why there are so many rules dealing with what might seem like very mundane matters. For example, some monks found a dead elephant and cooked and ate some of its flesh. People complained to the Buddha. They found it upsetting because of the cultural associations – the elephant was the royal animal. The Buddha made a minor rule forbidding the eating of elephant meat, not because it would prevent anyone from becoming enlightened but because it was socially unacceptable.

Rules are essential to prevent the order from acting in a way which would alienate the lay community. Rules are also essential for harmony within the order. The Vinaya lays down detailed procedures concerning monks' behaviour towards each other, thus reducing any friction that might arise within the community.

Once when the Buddha was on tour with a large group of monks, a few junior monks rushed ahead and reserved all the best lodgings for themselves. Sariputta, who was one of the Buddha's two foremost disciples, was forced to spend the night at the foot of a tree because there was nowhere else left for him to sleep. The Buddha reproved the junior monks.

He then asked the community who was most deserving of the best lodging, the best water, the best food. Some replied that it should be those monks who had been born into the Brahmin caste; others said those from the Kshatriya caste. Some suggested those well-versed in the Buddha's discourses; others said those skilled in concentration or advanced *vipassana* meditators.

The Buddha rejected all these suggestions. He said that the person who deserved the best – that is, the senior monk – was the one who had been in the order for the longest period of time.

Establishing such a hierarchy immediately removes the possibility of many of the intrigues that can weaken any group. As everyone in the order knows that seniority is solely based on time spent in the robe, there is little scope left for attempts to get to the top through underhand scheming.

★ ★ ★

There is a common view held in the West, based perhaps in Darwinian biology, that human beings have evolved mentally over the centuries, with the result that modern man is somehow more advanced. Although this view is less fashionable than it was, it still lingers.

One area in which it manifests are those groups who believe that spiritual ways such as *Buddhadhamma* need to be updated. I remember reading one article where the author stated that Buddhism was incomplete and would be improved by incorporating what he called the 'recent advances in child psychology'.

Something that becomes very clear from reading the Vinaya is that although social conditions change, human psychology does not. The stories in the Vinaya show human beings demonstrating the same range of behaviour – from the most petty and destructive to the most noble and compassionate – that humans perform today.

For example: a former minister had become a monk

and his wife had become a nun. On one occasion he was eating a meal in her presence. In the words of the Vinaya, 'Then that nun enticed that monk, standing near him with drinking water and with a fan as he was eating. Then that monk upbraided that nun, saying, "Do not, sister, do this, it is not allowable." She replied, "Formerly you did this and that to me, now you do not put up with this much," and having thrown down the drinking cup on his head, she struck him with the fan.'

★ ★ ★

In his very first discourse the Buddha stated that the way to enlightenment, the middle way, avoided the extremes of indulgence and self-mortification. So although the lifestyle of the monk is austere (and how austere one finds it depends on what one has been used to), it's not an extreme.

Ascetic practices were widespread in the India of the Buddha's day – indeed, he himself had followed that path for six years before recognising that it did not lead to enlightenment.

The rules the Buddha laid down reflected his rejection of extreme ascetic practices. One radical deviation from the ascetic tradition was that the Buddha allowed his monks and nuns to wear sandals, as opposed to having to go barefoot. He also made a rule forbidding monks and nuns to go naked, which was a common practice among ascetics.

The Buddha allowed his monks three robes. This is quite a lot by tropical standards, but it was the amount of clothing he had found was sufficient to keep warm even during the times of snowfall in northern India. As he said,

'Even those who in this *dhamma* and discipline are sons of respectable families, susceptible to cold, afraid of cold, even these are able to keep themselves going with three robes.'

On this very question of asceticism, the Buddha faced the most serious challenge to his authority.

The monk Devadatta (who was also the Buddha's cousin) had built up a following, which included the patronage of a prince, by showing off his psychic powers. It's said that 'overcome by gains, honours and fame, a longing arose in his mind, "It is I who will lead the order of monks".'

On an occasion when the Buddha was teaching a large group of monks, Devadatta approached and said, 'Lord, you are now old, worn, stricken in years, near the end of your life. Be content to live devoted to living in ease. It is I who will lead the order of monks.'

The Buddha told him, 'I, Devadatta, would not hand over the order of monks even to Sariputta or Moggallana. How then could I hand it over to you, a wretched one to be vomited like spittle?'

Incensed by this public humiliation, Devadatta determined to gain revenge. On several occasions he hired assassins and he even attempted to kill the Buddha himself. When all his attempts failed, Devadatta decided to try and split the order. With a group of his supporters he went to the Buddha with a list of five suggested improvements to the monastic lifestyle.

These were: that monks should always dwell in the forests (and should never stay in villages); that they should only obtain food from the almsround (and never accept invitations to meals); that they should always wear rag-robes, that is, robes made up from scraps of discarded cloth (as opposed to accepting robes from householders); that they should only live 'at the foot of a tree' and not be allowed any form of shelter; and, finally, that they should not eat fish or meat.

This was a shrewd political move on Devadatta's part; he was well aware, as it's put in the Vinaya, that 'people esteem austerity'.

The Buddha's response to Devadatta's suggestions was this: 'A monk may dwell in the forest or in a village, he can beg for alms or accept an invitation; he can, if he wishes, wear rag-robes. For eight months of the year lodging at the foot of a tree is permitted, and fish and flesh are allowable if it is not seen, heard or suspected that the animal has been killed specifically for the monk.'

Devadatta was secretly pleased that the Buddha rejected his five points. On the basis of this, he put it about that the Buddha's monks were soft and indulgent. Not long after, five hundred monks decided to follow him rather than the Buddha.

Note that Devadatta sought to split the order not by contradicting any of the Buddha's teaching but by trying to introduce a more ascetic lifestyle, something he saw would gain him support both from inside and outside the order.

People esteem austerity. Intriguingly, there are still those, for instance, who would like to smuggle vegetarianism into Buddhism in spite of everything the Buddha himself said on the subject. In the *Sutta Nipata* the Buddha gives a long list of actions which include stealing, adultery, lying, arrogance, conceit and deception; these, he says, are that which is disgusting, not the eating of flesh.

★ ★ ★

As you might expect, there are many, many rules designed to curb indulgence rather than self-mortification. Let's look at the rules concerning dress. On various occasions rules had to be made against the following: wearing red robes, black robes, robes with borders of flowers, jackets, turbans, robes made of bark, hair, antelope hide and even owls' wings.

Sometimes people assume that as the recluse only has a few material possessions he or she has little scope for material acquisitiveness. Simply becoming a monk or nun does not change anyone. If as a lay person someone has a lot of craving for material things, then as a recluse he or she transfers that craving on to monastic possessions.

The Buddha allowed his monks eight possessions: three robes, a begging bowl, razor, needle, belt and a water-strainer.

What sort of bowl might an acquisitive monk want? Well, rules had to be made forbidding the use of the following: gold bowls, silver bowls, bowls made of glass, bronze or copper, bowls decorated with pearls or beryl. One monk carried a bowl made from a skull, which terrified the lay people who thought he was a demon-worshipper.

The Buddha said that only bowls made of iron or clay were allowed. The Vinaya continues, 'Now at that time the bases of the bowls were scratched. They told this matter to the Buddha. He said, "I allow you, monks, a circular bowl-rest".'

One group of monks started using bowl-rests made of gold, of silver, and so on. Some even used bowl-rests carved with figures and symbols and toured around the locality showing them off. More rules were laid down.

There is an interesting story concerning a bowl made

of sandalwood. A merchant had placed it on top of a tall pole and he announced that anyone who could get it down by means of his psychic powers could keep it.

One of the Buddha's monks won this prize but, in doing so, he so impressed the onlookers that they all followed him back to his monastery. The Buddha, who was staying in this monastery, heard the commotion. He later rebuked the monk for misusing his powers. 'How could you, monk, exhibit a wonder of psychic power on account of a wretched wooden bowl?' This incident led to a rule being laid down that psychic powers were not to be exhibited to householders.

There are many episodes in the Vinaya which feature psychic powers - which is not really surprising given that many monks practised concentration meditation and many would have developed such skills. It's interesting to note how often such powers got monks into trouble. Psychic power is no different to any other power, in that it so often corrupts.

★ ★ ★

Some of the rules were formulated by the Buddha in response to incidents he witnessed himself; on other occasions he was prompted by reports from other monks. Rules were also laid down as a result of complaints from lay people.

In the early days of the order, for example, the monks were homeless and used to walk on tour throughout the year. When the rains came after the long dry season, crops were planted and vegetation sprouted up. People complained that the monks were trampling down the plants. The Buddha therefore instituted the rains retreat, a period during which monks had to stay within the confines of a monastery.

The order was totally dependent on the laity for support and so it had to be sensitive to cultural and social values. There was an occasion when monks ordained some warriors in the service of King Seniya Bimbisara. The generals were far from pleased. They reported the matter to the king, who asked his chief minister what the law said about those who ordain people who are in royal service. The minister said that the monks officiating at the ordination of such a person would have their heads cut off, their tongues torn out and half their ribs broken.

The king, concerned that monks should suffer such a fate, suggested to the Buddha that it would be best if the monks did not ordain anyone in the service of a king. The Buddha agreed and established a rule to that effect.

* * *

In Theravadin Buddhist countries, such as Burma and Thailand, monasticism has been of central importance; the monks have preserved the teaching. But just as the monastic system has been the backbone of Theravada Buddhism, so the Vinaya has been the backbone of the monastic system.

As we've seen, many of the rules are based in cultural considerations as opposed to ethical ones. When Buddhist monasticism comes to the West, it finds itself in a very different cultural climate. Two statements that the Buddha made are particularly relevant in this context.

Firstly, there's an incident in the Vinaya where some monks from the remote region of Avanti asked for dispensation to amend some rules because of the special local conditions. For example, in Avanti it was customary to bathe every day; if the monks didn't follow suit, they would not be thought well of. The Buddha said that the monks could bathe every day, even though this contradicted a previous rule. Several other exceptions to rules were made for monks in what were termed 'the outlying districts'.

The second incident occurred during the Buddha's final hours. He told Ananda that after his death the order could, if it so wished, abolish the minor rules.

These examples clearly show that the Buddha believed that some rules could be modified and even, if necessary, abandoned.

In the late 1980's, a new Buddhist order came into existence when two monasteries (for monks and nuns respectively) were founded in Wiltshire by Alan and Jacqui James.

The code of discipline established for the monks and nuns retained all the major rules of the Vinaya. New minor rules were drawn up which reflected the cultural conditions of late 20th-century Britain rather than those of ancient India. And so rules about things like the almsround and robes have been replaced with rules relevant to a modern western lifestyle. To retain a rule forbidding the eating of elephant meat, for example, is not exactly pertinent to the spiritual search.

One rather more notable change that was made, however, was that the nuns' rules were made identical with those of the monks. (Traditionally nuns had more rules than monks; the monks had 227 rules and the nuns an extra 50.) Again, laying down the same rules for recluses of both sexes reflects the context in which the new order finds itself.

But irrespective of any changes in the outward form, the purpose of the rules remains the same. They support the development of mindfulness and the restraint of craving and hatred, promote harmony within the group and help safeguard the teaching by discouraging behaviour which might bring it into disrepute.

In view of what the Buddha himself had to say about the rules, this modern expression is entirely consistent with the spirit of the Vinaya. The oriental cultural accretions have been left behind – all that remains is a code of discipline which gives the monk or nun the best possible foundation for treading the path to enlightenment.

Luminous Mystery

May 1989

'How can you hope to approach the truth through words?
It cannot be perceived subjectively or objectively. Full
understanding can only come to you through
an inexpressible mystery.'

Huang Po

Luminous Mystery

*L*ife and death, so all true spiritual ways tell us, are profoundly mysterious.

Buddhism presents us with paradoxes which at once tantalise and frustrate. It points to an ultimate reality beyond this scheme of things, a mysterious reality so far beyond this world that nothing definitive can be said about it. And yet at the same time it's present here-now and not separate from us.

But, for so many people, for so much of the time, life is perceived as being humdrum, predictable or just plain boring. At first sight this seems difficult to reconcile with all this profound mystery. Indeed, the ability to see life as tedious and uninspiring (which many manage to practise with considerable dedication) begins to seem like quite a feat; it begins to look like quite a mystery itself.

How is it that we come to deny mystery and manage to turn life into something grey and boring?

Perhaps what is most noticeable about people who moan about life being uninteresting is that they are not actually contacting the world; further, they don't even want to contact the world.

The person who is bored or depressed can only achieve that state by continually focusing on what he or she wants. He may want attention, affection, admiration, pain-free meditation or even a good night's sleep. By repeatedly comparing what he is actually experiencing with what he would like to experience, he maintains his dull grey mental state in being.

When people are obsessed with thoughts about all the things life isn't giving them, then their minds are closed to what is really happening. They could be in the midst of the most perfect spring day but, if they are totally caught up with themselves, their eyes will be closed to the dynamism and beauty of the new season. Such self-involvement negates the mystery and wonder of the world. It negates what the Buddha described as the luminous nature of mind.

Any form of self-involvement stains the mind. The Buddha listed four *asava* or stains, four different ways in which we corrupt the mind's natural luminosity. The four are: attachment to sensuality, attachment to becoming, attachment to view and ignorance.

However we classify the attachment, the result is always the same. Every time we reduce life to attachment to me and mine, then we create an impoverished world, a world devoid of mystery. And all this self-involvement not only impoverishes our own world but it also pollutes the worlds of all those with whom we come into contact.

In the case of the first *asava*, attachment to sensuality, we are preoccupied with gaining sensory gratification and become blinkered to the subtler aspects of life. Our minds are constantly filled with thoughts about food, sex, music, whatever. All that exists for us is the thought of pleasure, how I'm going to get it, how I'm going to hang on to it. And such concern is inevitably accompanied by a certain degree of fear - fear of not getting the pleasures we believe we need, fear of losing whatever pleasures we might have acquired. Buddhism states unequivocally that without craving, there can be no fear.

Some, rather than habitually focusing on immediate sensory gratification, choose instead to concentrate on more long-term goals. This is what Buddhism describes as becoming. We're never content with what is present but rather are convinced that satisfaction lies off in the future - when we're richer, more famous, more secure, wiser; when we're better people altogether.

In our obsession with directing our life along the channels that we consider worthwhile, everything is seen as a means towards an end. We're always thinking in terms of life **really** starting 'when ...'

But becoming is never-ending. Although we may not realise it, before one goal is realised we've already set up another.

There is an episode recounted by the biologist Lyall Watson which provides a striking illustration of both the third and fourth *asava*, attachment to view and ignorance.

It's well-known that certain plants produce chemicals such as tannin as a defence against the animals that feed on them. But scientists working in this area in Africa in the early '80s discovered something they found very strange. They found that not only does the specific plant being browsed quickly start producing its chemical defences, but that other plants in the immediate vicinity also start doing the same thing. Plants not in direct physical contact with the one being attacked show a sympathetic increase in tannin levels.

These scientists did not publish their findings in any scientific journal. They knew that none of the established journals would ever consider using anything so controversial.

What they came up against was attachment to view. The scientific world believes that the physical world operates according to certain established laws. One of these laws is that plants cannot communicate without something physical actually passing from one plant to another. To suggest otherwise - that plants might be aware, and capable of passing and receiving messages by some non-physical means - is to risk ridicule and derision. Such is often the fate of those working too far outside the boundaries of scientific orthodoxy.

Attachment to view and ignorance go hand in hand. Whenever you have fixed views about the world, then you have no choice but to ignore all evidence to the contrary if you wish to keep your views intact.

Scientists have often ignored what they regard as heretical ideas. Today this can be seen in the typical attitude of lay science towards psychic phenomena. In the face of considerable evidence to the contrary, it continues in a truly unscientific manner to dismiss the entire question on the assumption that psychic phenomena do not exist.

Irrespective of whether views are political, scientific or religious, attachment to them diminishes life's magic and beauty; the more rigid, limited and inaccurate the view, the more impoverishing it is. The person with a fixed view structure doesn't want life to contain things that cannot be readily explained: mystery has no place in his world.

* * *

Mind is luminous. Whenever we cease to cloud the mind with attachment to sensuality, ambition, dogma and dullness, we begin to recognise the fallacy of separation. Buddhism states that in reality there is no separation. We are not separate from the mystery of reality. At those times when we recognise this to be the case, life is incredibly vibrant and immediate.

But as soon as we believe in 'me in here experiencing life out there', then we move into the domain of self, with all its associated desires and comparisons. The beauty of the world is obscured beneath incessant mental chatter, so much of which deals with themes like, 'How can I get the most out of this?', 'What does this mean for me personally?' or 'Why should I have to put up with this?'

This domain of self is also the domain of time. Comparisons are made; ideas of past and future are introduced. Either we're looking back to a golden past or forwards to a glowing future. Because it doesn't immediately give us what we want, the moment is abandoned in favour of a dream.

In rejecting life as it is unfolding and choosing instead to live in a dream, we retreat from that which is truly mysterious - maybe even awesome and terrible - to a fantasy world that is in comparison one-dimensional and colourless.

Ironically, it's the fantasy that is predictable - it's

predictable because it's constructed from past experience. Fantasy can only ever be a re-ordering of things we've seen, heard or perceived before; fantasy deals solely with the known. Only in the absence of attachment is one dealing with the unknown, the moment, the real mystery.

★ ★ ★

Vipassana meditation undermines attachment. It destroys the very things that obscure life's mystery. Meditation is all about paying attention to what is really going on.

So much of the time, we interpret the things we see according to our preconceived ideas. We believe, for example, that we have some sort of permanent self, whereas Buddhism states that things are impermanent, unsatisfactory and ultimately beyond our control - non-self. And yet so often we unquestioningly believe them to be permanent, satisfactory and capable of being owned and manipulated; we see them as being me or mine. These three beliefs are known as the three *vipallasa* or hallucinations of perception.

Through meditation these *vipallasa* are eroded and gradually a more accurate view of the world is established. In this process we begin to discover that the universe is not the stable, dependable place we thought it to be.

We begin to see how creative mind actually is. We see that we each create our own world, which we then people with angels or devils and with harmony or strife. We see that everyone's world is quite unique and all experience personal.

The more we observe mind, the more familiar we become with its subtlety. Something that this greater familiarity reveals is the extent to which we are all affected by others on a mental level. We begin to discover that independence is a myth.

Whenever we feel isolated, the sense of myself is very prominent – 'me, separate from life out there'. Weakening this belief in a permanent self weakens the feeling of isolation. No longer caught up in self-concern, the mind is far more subtle and begins to notice nuances that were previously lost beneath the demands of the ego. Such nuances could be called intuition; they are part of the psychic side of the mind, which is always present but so often overlooked.

Tuning into psychic intimations involves learning to discriminate genuine intuition from wishful thinking. To do this successfully, we have to be at ease with the fact that life is so often mysterious – things can't always be explained. Often one knows something intuitively without being able to say how one arrived at such knowledge. And why should we always have to know how the mind got from A to Z? If we do not trust intuition without needing to understand it rationally, are we not saying, 'I won't accept it because I can't control it'? The need to control takes us back to the belief in a self and back to a limited universe.

★ ★ ★

Let's look at a couple of subjects on which for very good reasons the teachings of the Buddha make no comment, leaving two areas of mystery where other philosophical systems tend to make dogmatic statements.

Buddhism says nothing in answer to the question, 'Where did it all come from?'. There are no accounts of a first beginning of the world or of creator gods, no theories about random combinations of chemicals producing the first forms of life.

All the Buddha was concerned with was the condition in which beings find themselves. He said, 'There is *dukkha*' - there is unsatisfactoriness, and this unsatisfactoriness arises because we crave for things to be different from the way they are. No comment is made on the historical causes of this predicament. The reason for this is straightforward.

The Buddha was concerned solely with teaching a way to the complete cessation of suffering and therefore anything to do with formulating theories about first causes is irrelevant. The Buddha thoroughly described and analysed how we create suffering in the moment and how we can stop this process. His teaching is totally practical and is unconcerned with speculation; speculation is unhelpful in the quest for enlightenment.

A monk named Malunkyaputta once threatened to leave the order unless the Buddha gave him answers to a whole list of speculative questions, such as whether or not the universe was eternal. The Buddha told Malunkyaputta that he was like a man who had been shot and badly wounded by an arrow. Instead of letting the doctor treat him, he insisted that he first had to know who had shot the arrow, how tall he was, where he was from, the type of bow and bow-string he used, and so on.

The Buddha said he didn't deal with speculation for the simple reason that such questions are of no use on the quest for enlightenment; they are conducive to neither tranquillity nor wisdom.

Of course, there are some who are ill at ease unless they have a convenient answer for everything, and such people can feel threatened by the Buddha's silence on the subject of first beginnings. They are further discomfited when they find that the Buddha also made no comment on the state of the enlightened person after death. The reason for this silence is that on death the enlightened person has gone so far beyond this scheme of things that any statement that could be made would be inaccurate. Therefore Buddhism, being a rigorously logical system, keeps silence.

In keeping silent on these topics, Buddhism is implicitly stating that human rational understanding is limited and is incapable of a full comprehension of life. Contrast this position with that of traditional western science, which believed that everything could be known and measured and ultimately reduced to mechanistic laws.

Buddhism and other effective spiritual ways state that truth is beyond reason. Very loosely speaking, their position could be described as follows: we come from a mystery, we are surrounded by a mystery, we are ourselves a mystery and if we become enlightened, well - more mysteries are waiting.

Western materialism, on the other hand, claims that we are capable of understanding everything through science and that things not yet understood will one day be explained when more progress has been made.

These two world views produce very different attitudes towards life and living. The former position, the pro-mystery group, tends towards an attitude of reverence, of openness and of respect towards other forms of life. The second position, the anti-mystery group - who believe that a mystery only exists because there isn't enough data available - tends to see life in anthropocentric terms. They see humankind as the pinnacle of creation, better than all other forms of life. They are inclined to be manipulative, believing they can control and exploit the world by means of what they see as their superior brain power.

An attitude of openness is essential to the meditative path. In taking up meditation, one is making a statement that a materialistic lifestyle has not been sufficiently satisfactory.

One of the ways the meditator opens himself to mystery is by ceasing to rely on beliefs and by coming to examine all experience directly. If we have always believed, for example, that people are inherently untrustworthy, then we will perceive the world in those terms; we actually overlay an aura of suspicion on to the people we meet. If we suspend the belief and look at the facts, we find that in reality people exhibit all degrees of trustworthiness, from the greatest honesty to the most extreme deceit.

By giving up the attachment to such a blanket generalisation, our world immediately becomes less predictable, less familiar and much richer.

* * *

Through paying meditative attention, we come to see how subjective experience actually is. Each one of us constructs a personal reality through selective ignorance and the arbitrary interpretation of raw sense-data.

As the meditation practice unfolds and insight into impermanence is deepened, there comes a point where it is clearly seen that consciousness can only arise when the appropriate conditions are present. The meditator knows through his own experience that seeing, for example, can only arise through the combination of both the eye and a visual object. If either the eye or the visual object are absent or there is no contact between the two, then seeing cannot take place.

This insight reveals that things can only come to be with the appropriate combination of conditions and, moreover, that there doesn't need to be a self or soul somehow making things happen. It erodes the view that we are in control, the *vipallasa* of a controlling self. As this view is undermined, a new order of mystery is perceived. Without the belief in self, the world is seen to be infinitely more mysterious and awesome. Meditation reveals that all events are incredibly fleeting and only arise due to the coming together of an infinite number of conditions.

Let's look at seeing consciousness in more detail.

Seeing cannot take place without an eye and a visible object, which we'll say in this example is a tree. The tree needs to be within the range of the eye - seeing consciousness cannot arise if the tree is twenty miles away or if the eye is closed. There also needs to be light. The eye needs to be healthy and functioning, which means that the body to which it belongs also needs to be functioning. For the body to function, it has to have food and oxygen to breathe. Mental attention is also necessary - seeing can't take place if one is lost in daydream.

For the tree to exist there must be soil, the appropriate weather conditions and there must have been other trees to produce the seed from which it grew. For there to be the appropriate weather conditions, there need to be certain atmospheric conditions and the correct alignment of the earth in relation to the sun.

The Buddha said that to fully describe any one event one would inevitably have to describe the whole vast universe.

★ ★ ★

Mind arises and ceases an infinite number of times each day. And each time it is conditioned by the most complex inter-relationships. We are not separate from this process – in fact, perhaps it would be better to say that we **are** this process.

We each have an infinite wealth of past conditioning and at different times different aspects of that conditioning will be uppermost in our experience.

It is said that those skilled in the psychic power of recollecting past lives can develop the ability to recall literally thousands of existences. Given this, it seems narrow-visioned when people talk about their psychological difficulties being caused by what their parents did or didn't do to them when they were young. Such an outlook unquestionably belongs to the anti-mystery faction I spoke of earlier. So often with this psychiatric approach, the desire to understand the historical causes for a problem is really just an attempt to control it.

Whatever our parents did or did not do to us, inevitably we will experience painful feelings. A meditator tries to accept such feelings, knowing that they are completely unavoidable and recognising that what matters is his actions in the moment.

From the point of view of coming to enlightenment, whether feelings are painful or pleasant is irrelevant. All that is important is to avoid responding with self-concern. The meditator sees that life inevitably contains both pain and pleasure – there could not be one without the reference point of the other. He therefore realises the futility of trying to contrive a world of endless pleasure and is able to have respect, even reverence, for painful situations, rather than seeing them as simply unfair.

So many of our problems are caused by our limited

vision, our inability to see the wider picture beyond our immediate desires. When we think we know it all, the world is limited. And when we believe ourselves to be familiar with the world, that familiarity can breed contempt.

Those who expend great quantities of effort trying to keep life ordered and under control might like to consider the following. One teacher commented that when we die we look back on the experiences of this lifetime very much in the way that we look back on dreams when we wake after a night's sleep. Sometimes we hardly remember anything. Or perhaps we might just think, 'I wonder what that was all about.'

★ ★ ★

An old man died with no surviving relatives. The landlord of the flat the man had lived in knew that his tenant had been far from wealthy. Realising that it was highly unlikely that anything of value would be found amongst the man's belongings, the landlord had the flat cleared – everything was thrown out, no one even bothered to look through it.

Everything that means so much to us now will one day be forgotten, both by ourselves and by everyone else. There's therefore little point in taking any of our desires or beliefs too seriously.

The less time and effort we waste in the futile attempt to reduce the mystery of life to a familiar and comprehensible package labelled 'me and mine', the more vibrant and unpredictable life becomes and the less we suffer.

This is what the spiritual path is all about. And even the path itself is mysterious. For one thing, we don't know where we're going. If we did, we'd already be there. Every step along the path we're abandoning the known and opening ourselves to the mystery of the moment.

It is this mysterious quality of both the path and the goal that Carlos Castaneda's teacher was referring to when he said: 'Everything that surrounds us is an unfathomable mystery. We must try to unravel these mysteries, but without ever hoping to accomplish this. A warrior, aware of the unfathomable mystery that surrounds him and aware of his duty to try to unravel it, takes his rightful place among mysteries and regards himself as one.'

Against The Stream

September 1995

*It would be misleading to disguise the fact that the path
does inevitably involve giving things up.*

Against The Stream

*A*t the meditation centre we receive various Buddhist journals from around the world. The one that seems to arrive most frequently comes from Taiwan. It's well laid out and the quality of the paper and printing is good, but we haven't a clue about the content because it's all in Chinese.

We also get magazines from Malaysia and Thailand but, in my opinion, by far the most entertaining come from the United States. They are not particularly interesting because of the articles – what makes them so fascinating is the adverts.

There are adverts for a Buddhist summer school, where small groups of 9-12-year-old boys can learn, amongst other things, meditation, woodsmanship and playing the bagpipes. Or you could subscribe to a magazine 'for those interested in Buddhism and the Grateful Dead'. (Indeed the merchandising of Buddhism seems not so very different from that of a rock group with all the T-shirts and pendants there are for sale.) There are adverts for property. You could buy an ocean-side estate complete with those two essentials that no American Buddhist should be without – a hot tub and a stupa. Or you could buy a Tibetan Terrier – 'holy dogs' as the advert says.

There are usually several companies advertising exotic holidays, though they never use the word holiday. They call the trips 'pilgrimages' or 'spiritual journeys', and the destination is usually somewhere like a recently opened-up, remote Himalayan valley. Once there you can put on your meteorite jewellery and embark on a gender-neutral wilderness journey to commune with the sacred goddess.

★ ★ ★

There are many Buddhist journals available today, some of a very high standard. Some of these journals devote themselves solely to articles on the Buddha's teaching. But many readers want Buddhist journals to cover a much wider spectrum of topics, they prefer a more eclectic approach. Such people want to see articles on politics, poetry and ecology, they want recipes and a gardening column and so on.

A journal that satisfies this market will of course be far more successful commercially, but there is always the danger that by going down this particular road it will end up as just another magazine catering for the well-heeled, slightly alternative, politically-correct set looking for the latest in ethnic chic.

Articles on *dhamma* itself will only appeal to a very small audience; the teaching is against the stream.

The Buddha described the *dhamma* as 'deep, difficult to see, difficult to understand, subtle'. He described the world as 'delighting in sensual pleasure, delighted by sensual pleasure, rejoicing in sensual pleasure'. If you want a Buddhist magazine to sell well, then you reduce the number of articles on the teaching and increase the number of articles on sense pleasures.

The way of the world is essentially one of addition. We seek happiness through craving, we seek happiness through adding things to our life - possessions, relationships, experiences. The pages of Buddhist magazines are not exempt from this same acquisitiveness. And so the teaching itself becomes just another lifestyle accessory, something people can add to their lives in the form of an exotic hobby or a spiritually advanced pet.

In contrast, enlightenment is not something we can gain, it's not something we can add on to our experience. 'I truly attained nothing,' the Buddha said, 'from complete, unexcelled enlightenment.'

Enlightenment is the total cessation of suffering, something which is always available but which we ignore. It's compared to the sun hidden by cloud: it's there but we cannot see it. But we only have to get rid of the clouds, we don't have to create a sun.

Thus the path to enlightenment is essentially one of getting rid of things. We work at eliminating craving, hatred and ignorance, eliminating views, attachments and all the things that perpetuate suffering and hide enlightenment. In a very real sense, the path gives us nothing; it is simply the abandoning of wrong ideas.

It is this theme of abandoning, of giving up, that I want to look at tonight.

There is a word that encapsulates this quality but it is one of those terms associated with the path that can suddenly make people feel rather drowsy. I did originally consider trying to think up a more positive-sounding synonym, but the problem with such terms is that they take us back into the idea of the path giving us things and making us better people. And anyway it would be misleading to disguise the fact that the path does inevitably involve giving things up. The word I have in mind is renunciation.

Traditionally renunciation (*nekkhamma* in Pali) refers specifically to freeing oneself of sensual desires, but in this lecture I want to talk about renunciation in its broadest sense; I want to talk about the renunciation of all the things we do which keep us tied to *samsara*, all those things we do which cloud enlightenment.

Renunciation, in one form or another, is essential to all aspects of the Buddha's eightfold path. To the non-meditator it sounds unattractive - indeed to many meditators it sounds unattractive. And it is because of this that writers of the more populist Buddhist books usually just skirt around the subject.

Renunciation is most definitely against the stream, but anyone who starts to meditate must have begun to suspect that following that particular stream only leads to suffering. I want to illustrate how renunciation is central to the reduction of negativity and thus how such renunciation is a wholly positive action.

★ ★ ★

In one of the discourses (or suttas) in the Pali Canon, there is a list of five similes describing the sense of freedom experienced by the meditator who has learned to put aside what are known as the hindrances. The hindrances are mental actions which we habitually perform and which obstruct meditative observation; basically, they are five expressions of selfishness: sensual desire, ill-will, sloth and torpor, agitation and doubt.

Freedom from the hindrances is likened to having paid off a debt, having recovered from a disease, having been let out of prison; it is likened to freedom after having been bound in slavery, and to reaching safety after travelling through a dangerous district. The fact that the Buddha used as many as five similes suggests that we tend to underestimate just how important it is to remove negative conditions.

Many people attempt to overcome mental distress by trying to overlay the problem with a positive attitude. This approach may well work in the short term but, because the roots of the negativity have not been addressed and understood, it cannot be a final solution. Dealing directly with existing negative conditions is certainly more challenging and harder work but it gives us the opportunity to develop real understanding.

Without renunciation the hindrances cannot successfully be overcome. Of course, renunciation is not all that is needed. To overcome the hindrances we need the correct balance of mental factors such as concentration, investigation and mindfulness. But there are many occasions on which renunciation is crucial.

There are many times, for example, when we have, consciously and deliberately, to decide not to pursue a particular daydream. When we have to say to ourselves that we will not plan – yet again – how to spend the winnings from our imminent national lottery success ... When we have to refuse to replay mentally an occasion on which we were, we believe, unjustly criticised ... When we have to decide that we really should continue to work at the meditation rather than give ourselves a little break for a few minutes ...

Such decisions are central to the real task of meditation. They are hard work, unglamorous and, especially in the early days, can seem quite thankless. This is far removed from the blissed-out image of meditation that so many people have, but all effective forms of meditation start with the process of learning how to overcome hindrances. Learning to overcome hindrances means repeatedly confronting the ego, which is a messy business.

Renunciation is necessary even to start on the path. If the path is taught properly, then the new meditator will be instructed in the precepts and how to keep them. For some, living by the precepts might not involve many changes in behaviour – maybe they only have to make minor adjustments like, say, no longer using slug pellets in their garden. For others, keeping the precepts might involve a radical change in lifestyle and a far greater degree of renunciation, as in the case of those whose social life had previously revolved around the consumption of large amounts of alcohol.

Finding the time to meditate regularly also involves renunciation. Especially for those with an already busy lifestyle, creating the time for meditation means foregoing other activities – maybe cutting down on socialising or, in the case of those who decide to get up a little earlier in the morning to fit in their meditation, renouncing that extra bit of sleep.

If someone is serious, there is also another, more subtle form of renunciation involved in learning to meditate, and that is the renunciation of the belief that he or she knows all about meditation and the spiritual path.

If someone seeks instruction, then he is tacitly acknowledging the possibility that someone else might know more than he does himself. This might sound obvious but it is surprising how many people ask to be taught but still act in a way that shows that they believe they know more than the instructor.

The renunciation of doing things 'my way' is central to the spiritual path. The importance of discipline and obedience is emphasised in all spiritual traditions whether in terms of surrendering to the will of God or as surrender to the guru. After all, anyone starting out on the spiritual path has, on one level, already seen that doing things their way has not produced total, lasting satisfaction.

If someone is capable of putting to one side their attachment to doing things their way and following the instruction of a skilled teacher, then all sorts of things are possible. On the other hand, if someone just clings to their attachments and views, then they get nowhere with the meditation and usually give up fairly soon, no matter how good the teacher.

Between these two extremes, most meditators are selective about their attachments and how much they are prepared to acknowledge and work on them.

Perhaps people decide that keeping four out of the five precepts is sufficient for them, or that they personally do not need to practise *metta*. In both of these cases there is an area of life where the meditator is not prepared to practise renunciation. It is these attachments which sooner or later prevent progress and the meditator finds that he gets stuck.

If these attachments are relatively coarse - by which I mean, for example, refusing to keep a precept - then very little progress can be made. If they are more subtle - like, say, an attachment to deeply concentrated states - then the meditator might progress a fair way along the path before coming to a halt.

Of course, none of these obstacles is permanent. What usually happens is that the meditator sees how renunciation in other areas of life has been positive and has brought great benefits, and so he is prepared to consider giving up the attachment that is obstructing progress.

* * *

Renunciation is necessary throughout the course of the meditative path. In the early days, as we attempt to meditate regularly, we soon discover that it is not always easy. We are instructed not to finish the meditation session before the alarm goes off; we are told, once settled, not to move. We are told that if our nose runs then we just leave it alone and observe.

If people follow these instructions then they will learn a lot but, in order to follow them successfully, they have to practise renunciation. They have to put to one side the desire to experience only interesting objects and the desire not to experience pain or discomfort. Whenever we move during the meditation or end it prematurely, then we lose an opportunity to learn. At such times we just strengthen self-concern.

If you think about it, not moving when you experience a persistent pain in the meditation is a very radical action.

It goes completely against the grain. We are conditioned to move away from pain and to move towards pleasure. Indeed, most of the world believes that an attachment to pleasure is natural and automatic.

If, during meditation, we resist the desire to scratch some annoyingly irritating sensation, we can learn many things. We learn that the world doesn't fall apart just because we do nothing to get rid of pain. We can see that the pain itself isn't necessarily the most prominent object - what our attention is more caught up with are the thoughts about that pain. We see that the pain appears to fluctuate and, although we believe that it is a very strong object, we still find it difficult to hold the mind on the pain. We see that it is as fickle as any other object of meditation.

It also becomes clear that any reaction to a painful feeling - such as moving or becoming irritated - is chosen. We begin to see that actions performed in response to feelings are volitional, they are not automatic. They only appear to be automatic in the absence of attentiveness.

For a meditator seeing this clearly for the first time, there are all sorts of ramifications. His outlook can be transformed by the revelation that he is totally responsible for his own actions. Whilst he may have previously appreciated this intellectually, he now knows that no situation can ever force him to act in a set way.

All this can be seen because a meditator resisted the desire to move. But such an act of renunciation also helps create the conditions for a meditator to see an even more important aspect of reality - it allows him to deepen his perception of transience.

He can see that pain is transient, disappearing many

times during even one minute. The physical sensation itself is transient, composed of the most fleeting moments of what *Buddhadhamma* calls earth, fire and air - in other words, fleeting experiences of pressure, temperature and motion. All feelings and perceptions associated with the experience are transient, as are all the thoughts and worries. The most melodramatic thoughts he can muster are transient, as are the hard-won moments of acceptance.

The path begins and ends with paying attention to transience. Learning to pay attention - learning to meditate - is, as my teacher often says, learning what not to do. We have to learn to stop doing all those things which prevent us from seeing clearly, and an important part of that learning process is the practice of renunciation.

★ ★ ★

There is a very close relationship between renunciation and giving. To give properly, we have to renounce ownership, we have to renounce the desire to keep something for ourselves. This applies just as much whether the gift is a physical object or perhaps a gift of our time.

If someone gives you something but shows a persistent interest in what you do with it - like the friend who gives you an item of clothing and then keeps asking you when you're going to wear it - then, from the meditative viewpoint, it is hardly a gift at all. When a meditator gives something he should truly give it away. If he has truly given it away, then he knows that what the recipient chooses to do with it is absolutely none of his business.

The Buddha once told his monks to become his 'heirs of *dhamma*, not heirs of material things'. He went on to describe how one monk, although tired and hungry, on hearing this instruction decided to renounce a meal. That action, he said, would 'for a long time conduce to that monk's desirelessness, to his contentment, to his being easily supported, to his putting forth energy'.

Occasionally foregoing a meal, or a favourite television programme, or a new garment, can have a very powerful effect on the mind. When we do such things, we are making a very definite statement to ourselves about our priorities. Such actions can have great symbolic importance.

In case you were wondering, this is not falling into the extreme of self-mortification, which the Buddha described as 'painful, unworthy, unprofitable'. The person who indulges this extreme has lost sight of the fact that renunciation is a means and not an end. He has forgotten that the purpose of giving things up is to overcome selfishness and attachment and instead has become selfishly attached to that giving up. He uses renunciation to bolster the ego rather than to undermine it.

Transference of merit is another aspect of renunciation. This is the practice of symbolically giving away the positive results of efficient action. It is a good idea at the start of an hour's meditation to dedicate the merit that accrues from the practice to someone else. Equally, when you give a gift, you can give away the merit you will earn from your generosity. This is a further refinement of renunciation, where one is not only giving up something physical but also renouncing all claim to the benefits of that action.

There are many other areas where we have to practise renunciation on the mental level. Here are some of them.

We have to renounce the desire always to be right. We have to renounce the desire to justify ourselves and to indulge in feeling offended. Maybe we have to renounce the desire for recognition or for a following. We have to renounce the past, which is after all only an idea. This means renouncing attachment to things done earlier in this lifetime, negative or positive, or indeed attachment to ideas of things done in previous lives. Whether they happened or not doesn't really matter.

One aspect of this renunciation of the past is the letting go of ideas about previous meditative accomplishment (or lack of it). Some meditators might become complacent and lazy because they cling to some past success, real or imaginary, in the practice. Or some might cling on to the view that their practice will always be difficult or painful. And with such an idea in their minds they usually make sure that it comes true. Or there are those meditators who have worked hard with the practice and established a certain level of calm and clarity – and then do all they can to maintain that state.

The path is about overcoming all attachments, including attachments to such things as calm and clarity. The meditative path is very dynamic but the more we interfere with the practice, the more we keep producing similar types of experience.

We can only find the practice consistently dull or consistently painful or consistently anything else because that is what we have chosen to create. Mind is ever-changing and it is the nature of the meditation practice to develop and to move into new areas. Stages marked by calm and clarity come and go, as do those marked by weak concentration or thoughts of futility.

Those clinging to calm and clarity do not let the mind move into new areas. As soon as the practice shows signs of becoming less clear, they pour in lots of energy to re-establish what they regard as a 'good' meditative state. What such meditators fail to understand is that the essence of the practice is the observation of transience, not the use of control to establish and maintain clarity. All things are transient: mindfulness is transient, clarity is transient, confusion, pain, sleepiness – all are transient.

Some meditators, on hearing about the various stages on the path of meditation, imagine there to be a neat linear progression in the practice. But there are times when a particular stage breaks up and then the meditation becomes very unfocused until the mind settles into the next stage. So the meditator not allowing the mind to move away from clarity into anything more chaotic is effectively preventing the progress of insight.

★ ★ ★

The lifestyle of the recluse inevitably involves considerable renunciation. A monk or nun has renounced relationships, career, possessions and leisure. In some traditions, recluses also renounce their name. In India the ceremony by which someone becomes a *sannyasin* includes an enactment of their own funeral, which marks the symbolic death of the person who is leaving the worldly life.

A few years ago a man who had taken *sannyas* decided to give it up and return to his old life. His family, who had got used to life without him, refused to have him back. He ended up going to the courts to try and regain his property. The judge ruled that he had no right to any of it; after all, he had completely renounced his past and thus the person who had once owned the property no longer existed.

Someone entering the Buddhist order renounces past status. A newly ordained monk or nun is the lowest in the hierarchy irrespective of social background. There is a story in the Canon about some Sakyan princes wishing to become monks who specifically asked to be ordained after a man who had previously been their barber. They recognised that being junior to someone from one of the lowest caste backgrounds would help them overcome their pride.

A monk or nun may have left behind many aspects of worldly life and chosen a lifestyle ideally suited to pursuing the spiritual path, but they still have to practise renunciation. Just because a monk or nun has given up relationships, career and so on doesn't mean that they have given up attachment to those things. Hatred and craving can never be overcome by the manipulation of one's physical surroundings, no matter how skilled. Renunciation of physical actions is, by itself, never enough.

* * *

The Buddha said that any object that arises, in mind or body, should 'by perfect intuitive wisdom be seen as it really is, thus: This is not mine, this I am not, this is not myself'. No pain, feeling, memory, idea or ideal needs to be grasped at and identified with. Anything we become aware of, however alluring or repulsive, however overwhelming or subtle, we can label as 'not mine, not me, not myself'.

This is one of the subtlest levels of renunciation, where we are consciously and systematically renouncing ownership and control.

Seeing things as 'not me, not mine, not myself' is a corrective to the view of self; a corrective to the view that there is within us something unique, unchanging and independent; a corrective to the view that we can own and manipulate things. It is exactly analogous to the way that we train ourselves to see transience as a corrective to the view we hold that things are permanent.

And just as the systematic noting of transience produces insight into *anicca*, so the systematic noting of the 'not mine, not me, not myself' nature of things produces insight into *anatta*. Through insight, our understanding of *anicca*, *anatta* and *dukkha* is radically changed from something that we are trying our best to point out to ourselves, to something we **know**. Through insight, understanding of *anicca*, *dukkha* and *anatta* becomes as it were encoded into our very approach to life. It is this insight which reduces and eliminates ignorance, craving and hatred. The more insight we gain, the less we suffer.

★ ★ ★

So what are the benefits of renunciation? In a word, freedom. Renouncing selfish physical actions brings freedom from guilt; renouncing selfish mental actions brings freedom from hindrances. Renouncing self-view frees us from always having to be right, frees us from having to maintain an image and from all of the limitations that having an image involves.

Renouncing hatred and craving frees us from dependency. Whenever we crave we make the megalomanic statement that there are specific things we **have** to experience. Craving is self-obsession and when we have such an obsession we care for no one but ourselves. If we are obsessed with ideas of what we think we need, we are always going to be, to some degree, treacherous.

Renunciation of the belief that we are the centre of the universe, and that we are or should be special or better or worse than others, brings freedom from so many of the actions that corrupt our world and the worlds of those around us.

And finally, the perfection of renunciation, along with the perfection of all aspects of the eightfold path, brings freedom from birth and death, freedom from all suffering.

Life offers all sorts of treasures – riches, fame, excitement, successful relationships; we can, if we wish, dedicate our lives to any of these. Given enough time, we can experience them all. They all cost us a lot in terms of effort, determination and so on. The more worthwhile we find something to be, the more it costs us. The greatest treasure, enlightenment, has a price tag which reads 'This will cost you everything'. How many of us are prepared to pay the price?

Paradox

September 1994

The path uses craving to overcome craving and selfishness to overcome selfishness. The path doesn't produce enlightenment but without it enlightenment is not possible.

Paradox

A student was attending a lecture on his first day at
college. He began to notice that the person sitting
next to him was feeling very uncomfortable. She was
fidgeting around a lot, she kept dropping her notes and
was obviously in some distress. Suddenly, interrupting the
lecturer, she blurted out, 'Is it all right if I sit by the door?
I get claustrophobia.'

The lecturer said that was OK and so she picked up
her notes and shuffled over towards the door. But instead
of sitting near the door she actually sat down on the floor
just outside the room in a very small entrance hall. From
there she stuck her head around the door and continued
to listen to the lecture.

When it was over the student went over and asked her
why, if she suffered from claustrophobia, she had chosen

to sit in such a confined space. She answered, 'Well, I
suffer from agoraphobia as well.'

Tonight I want to talk about paradox. The dictionary
defines a paradox as a statement which on the face of it
seems self-contradictory, absurd or at variance with
common sense, though on investigation it may prove to be
essentially true.

It's both self-contradictory and yet essentially true that
we both want truth and yet don't want truth. Truth is
both the ultimate promise and the ultimate threat. A
famous Sufi mystic called Hallaj was tortured and killed
simply for stating, 'I am the Truth'. Throughout history
enlightened teachers have been both respected and perse-
cuted. Man's attitude to truth is highly ambivalent. On an
individual level, we all want truth and yet if someone
offers us a direct way to truth we often make excuses. 'I
can't follow it just yet because ...'

There are people who are quite conscious, on one
level, of their reluctance to commit themselves to truth
but who don't want to admit it. There are those whose
commitment has waned. For example, it is not
uncommon for monks wishing to disrobe to suddenly
discover an ailing parent they have to look after.

Perhaps one of the best escapes from truth is religion.
Someone once said that the art critic was man's revenge
against creativity. To plagiarise, I'd suggest that religion is
man's revenge against true spirituality.

A direct path to truth is, like everything else, transient.
If a path attracts a lot of followers it will also attract those
seeking worldly goals such as status or recognition.
Sooner or later the original teaching is corrupted. Bits of
the teaching are edited out or new bits added according
to the whims of the religious establishment.

One of the main reasons why Buddhism has avoided many of the worst excesses of religion is the Buddha's genius in laying down a comprehensive monastic discipline. Wealth and politics are basically off-limits to monks and nuns. But as over the centuries a religion grew up around the original teaching, there have arisen certain ideas contrary to the original spirit of the teaching (and certainly not to be found in the Pali Canon).

For example, it is said that an enlightened person can only survive for seven days as a lay person. Another erroneous concept is that it is only possible to become enlightened when there is an historic Buddha alive. Any such idea, which makes the attainment of enlightenment either more remote or even impossible, gives people the perfect excuse not to work. It allows them to carry on believing that they want truth without ever having to put that belief to the test.

An enlightened teacher puts us in a very difficult position because we are forced, on one level, to acknowledge whether we seriously want to do something about becoming enlightened or not. For those who would rather just be associated with the teaching, seeing it as an exotic hobby, but who do not actually want to give anything up, an enlightened teacher is far too threatening. They are much better off with a group whose central interest in Buddhism is aesthetic or academic.

But what if we do decide that our desire for freedom and truth is stronger than our desire to remain as we are? What if we decide that we are at last ready to work systematically to overcome fear, insecurity and self-interest? If we decide we do want truth, we then have to acknowledge and come to understand all those areas of life where we don't want truth. We have to look at all those lingering ideas of what we believe to be satisfactory in the world - family relationships, concentrated states, perhaps a group of adoring disciples.

Some more paradoxes. On the spiritual path we do lots of actions to discover that ultimately doing doesn't work and that it cannot bring enlightenment. We do to learn how to stop doing. On the spiritual path we become more disciplined and as a result we become freer. On the path we do lots of work on ourselves and we become less self-concerned. We learn that giving things away makes us richer. We abandon frivolity and we begin to see just how funny we actually are.

Truth is beyond words and logic. Because it is beyond words, whenever words are used to try and encompass truth they are in some way incomplete. Because logic cannot contain truth, at some point a description of truth will introduce statements that are mutually exclusive - in other words, it will contain paradoxes.

You've all heard it said many times that all things are transient but have you considered that that fact is always true? That the fact of transience is not itself transient?

There is a central paradox concerning the existence or not of a path to enlightenment. Some teachers state that enlightenment cannot be taught, whilst others state that there is indeed a path to enlightenment. Such opposing statements have given lots of ammunition to scholars and those who love to speculate and argue but, even though the statements appear to be contradictory, they are in fact both true.

Enlightenment, in the words of the Buddha, is 'the unborn, the uncreated, the unbecome'. It cannot be produced. If it could be produced its existence would be dependent on conditions. It would be transient and, as the

Buddha pointed out, anything transient is ultimately unsatisfactory. As someone once noted, if enlightenment could be produced it could be sold.

Enlightenment cannot be taught but the Buddha taught a way to enlightenment. Enlightenment is the beyond. It is beyond description, but teachers from the Buddha himself through to enlightened teachers of our own times have given us whatever descriptions they could to help us direct our endeavours most effectively.

We hear that enlightenment is closer to us than the air we breathe. The books tell us that *samsara* and *nibbana* are the same thing. We hear that we are, in fact, already enlightened. But because we don't believe or understand these things we need a path.

The path leads to a massive reduction in craving and hatred, a massive reduction in suffering. But it doesn't produce enlightenment. What it does produce is the experiential understanding that enlightenment cannot be produced. Ultimately the path shows us that no matter how mindful or concentrated or wise we become, we still cannot become enlightened through our own efforts. With that knowledge, it at last becomes possible for the meditator truly to let go; with that letting go, there is enlightenment.

We could say that we need the path to show us that we don't need a path. We need to meditate to discover that we don't need to meditate. Knowing we don't need a path it becomes possible to wake up and see enlightenment - in the laconic words of Huang Po, 'to know that that which is before you is it'.

There is a *sutta* in the Pali Canon (Middle Length Sayings 24) which lists all the stages of meditation from beginning to end, including the highest attainments and deepest insights that meditation can bring.

The *sutta* states very clearly that none of these attainments is 'utter *nibbana* without attachment'. But it goes on to say that neither can there be enlightenment without these attainments. Thus we have this central paradox that the path does not produce enlightenment but without the path enlightenment is not possible.

★ ★ ★

There are many other paradoxes associated with the path. To start right at the beginning, the basic qualification needed by anyone wishing to walk the path is sanity. In following the path one gradually overcomes self-importance, self-concern; one eventually sees that the whole issue of self was just a wrong idea.

But in order to even start on the path, the prospective meditator must have a strong and, in conventional terms, reasonably healthy self-image. It is paradoxical that for many they have first to strengthen their self-image before they can ever begin to understand and overcome it.

The spiritual path is not a refuge for those who cannot cope with the world. Anyone who is very neurotic or is in some other way mentally disturbed needs first to address those problems through such methods as psychotherapy.

For example, someone once came along to the centre wanting to take up meditation. He was so obsessed with his own hypochondria, his mind was so filled with thoughts about his physical well-being (or the lack of it), that he was unable to pay attention to anything else. When such a person has managed to come to terms with their psychological problems, meditation becomes possible.

Psychotherapy and the eightfold path do not overlap. Put simply, psychotherapy ends with sanity – which is the necessary starting-point for Buddhist training. There is a lot of confusion over this issue and a lot of people have tried, for instance, to integrate therapy and *vipassana* meditation. But no matter how clever or persuasive someone's argument, psychotherapy cannot lead to spiritual insight and *vipassana* as an isolated practice cannot cure mental illness.

Perhaps some of the confusion in this area has come about because some teachers have taught *vipassana* incorrectly. They have sought to divorce *vipassana* from its Buddhist context, treating it as purely an exercise in mind control. But *vipassana* is part of an integrated path to enlightenment; it is not the whole of the path. To be effective, *vipassana* must be taught within a framework which is grounded on the precepts and comprises the whole of the eightfold path.

There are those who talk about the need to go into therapy to explore emotional issues that come up in the meditation practice. One such issue – so strongly emphasised in the last few years that for some it has become something of an icon – is anger. Those coming to meditation from a therapeutic/counselling background often give anger a significance which is completely unjustified. They believe both that it has to be expressed and that its historic roots should be 'worked through'.

From the Buddhist perspective, anger is just another inefficient mental habit, neither more nor less significant than boredom, self-pity or stinginess. (Although you don't often hear about people going into therapy to discover why they are so reluctant to spend money on anyone but themselves ...)

The eightfold path is a way to the ending of all distress – it does not need augmenting with other practices. *Vipassana* meditation alone is not enough. But *vipassana* – when combined with the precepts, study, service, *metta* (loving-kindness) and generosity, and practised under expert instruction – does form a complete path to enlightenment.

The importance of *metta*, especially, should never be underestimated. No matter what actions someone might have performed in the past, no matter what others might have done to them, the practice of loving-kindness cannot fail to improve the way they feel about themselves. But remember that if *metta* is to succeed, it must be practised towards oneself. An hour's *metta* – beginning with the development of thoughts of friendliness towards oneself – is of infinitely greater value to the meditator than any amount of psychotherapy.

The Buddha said that throughout the world there is nothing more dear to people than themselves, and yet it is very common for meditators to find it difficult to do *metta* towards themselves. Thus we have the paradox that whilst on the one hand self-love is the very driving force of *samsara*, on the other very few people are prepared to love themselves.

Is it not the case that most people's self-love usually amounts to just giving themselves pleasure? Most people would not deny themselves comfort and pleasurable feelings (a fact both well-known to and thoroughly exploited by advertisers) but would feel resistance if they had to recollect their own positive qualities. If we cannot love ourselves how can we ever love another? And, if we equate love of ourselves solely with pleasure and indulgence, doesn't that mean that, in the same way, our love of others cannot go beyond giving them pleasant feelings? Success in *metta* is an essential component of the path to enlightenment and it cannot be achieved if we do not practise *metta* towards ourselves.

* * *

All spiritual ways emphasise obedience and discipline. To become enlightened we need to give up attachment to our own way of doing things. We also need to give up attachment to our beliefs, to our loves and hates. Thus, paradoxically, we need to give up attachment to our personalities in order to become truly ourselves.

Only the enlightened person is truly him- or herself. Before enlightenment our actions are full of 'shoulds' and 'should nots' and 'oughts' and 'ought nots'. We carry around a self-image which we try to live up to and which we persistently defend. We judge, censor or ignore thoughts and feelings that don't fit with our current self-image.

Only the enlightened person is totally accepting and at ease with himself. He accepts all aspects of his internal conditioning and knows that any personality has a whole range of responses; that in some areas those responses will be skilled, in other areas they won't. He knows that any thoughts or emotions that arise are perfect as they are, and that that perfection is utterly beyond any mundane judgement about the appropriateness or otherwise of such mental events.

The enlightened person is completely harmless; this is what Taoists refer to as perfect virtue. Such virtue transcends all considerations of good and evil. But to get to the point where it is possible to go beyond good and evil, one needs to understand and act in accordance with *sila* or ethics. So we have the paradox that in order to go beyond ethics first we have wholeheartedly to embrace a highly ethical lifestyle, seeing, in the words of the Canon, 'danger in the slightest faults'.

On one level, ignorance, hatred and craving are complex actions. They are all volitional; they all involve constructing and then maintaining a world that is highly egocentric. Mindfulness, on the other hand, is an exercise in simplicity. It simply requires being in the body, in the moment, observing things arise and pass away.

One meditator told me about a fantasy he had indulged in during a recent meditation. He had been involved in a plane crash and had heroically and single-handedly rescued many of the other passengers from the tangled wreckage. Adventure, romance, fame – we have all had the dreams.

Constructing such daydreams takes a lot of effort and is a highly creative activity. We can create the most complex and colourful of situations within seconds. Compare the fantasy of hauling rich and glamorous survivors from a smashed Concorde with the reality of being in the body noting the transience of bending, stretching, pressure, temperature.

If we say that the path is a process of simplification, then enlightenment is the ultimate simplicity. The enlight-ened person is spontaneous; he or she does not act in such a way as to maintain some image or to live up to some ideal. As the Canon says, 'There is no more of being such or such' – in other words, their actions are completely free of any idea that there is some sort of self that is acting.

Paradoxically, the being caught up in craving and hatred, with their attendant neuroses and paranoias, is very predictable, whilst the enlightened man or woman, whose mental universe is free from all such complexities, is utterly unpredictable.

The actions of the *puthujjana*, the untrained worldly person, are so predictable because no matter how intriguing or bizarre the content of his cravings and hatreds, you can bet everything you own on the fact that the central theme of all his fantasies is himself and what he wants.

The actions of the enlightened person are spontaneous and free; free of psychological baggage, free of all dependence. Again, to quote the Canon, 'They are trackless, like birds in the sky'. Being free of attachment, their actions do not conform to worldly patterns and expectations, and they cannot be predicted. The enlightened person no longer suffers but only he sees suffering in its totality.

* * *

To become enlightened we have to accept both our masculine and our feminine sides. Everyone has both aspects of mind. If someone values one aspect at the expense of the other, then he is divided against himself and the full development of wisdom and compassion is not possible.

Accepting both the masculine and the feminine does not, of course, mean that the meditator becomes some sort of androgynous being, occupying a middle ground between masculinity and femininity. Paradoxically, only when both masculinity and femininity are fully accepted does the individual become truly male or truly female.

Think of a young man who has always been at ease with his masculine side but has tended to shy away from the feminine. Circumstances arise which place him in a situation where he has to adopt a more caring, nurturing role - perhaps through fatherhood or through having to look after a sick friend or relative.

Developing that feminine side he becomes more complete, he becomes stronger. In learning not to be afraid to express the feminine side of his nature, he actually becomes more confident of his masculinity and more in tune with himself as a man; that is, after all, the sex which he has chosen to learn the lessons of this lifetime.

Of course, it might be that a man is already at ease with his feminine side but is estranged from the masculine. I recently came across the acronym SNAG - sensitive new age guy. All tai chi and sandals. For such people, developing the masculine is necessary before they can meditate effectively.

I've used two male examples but exactly the same principles apply to women. A woman might be alienated from either her feminine or her masculine side. Both women and men need to accept femininity and masculinity in order to develop spiritually. Chauvinism has no place in the mind of the meditator.

★ ★ ★

An issue of great importance to meditators is that of establishing the correct level of meditative effort. Some meditators simply don't try hard enough; they drift through the meditation, they take it easy and enjoy lots of daydreams. But more frequently meditators use too much effort and cause themselves considerable pain and distress. This is hardly surprising given our cultural bias towards hard work, striving and ambition, but when it comes to meditative effort the equation 'more equals better' simply doesn't apply.

In meditation we need to be more concerned with the quality of effort, rather than with the quantity of effort. Right meditative effort is gentle; it's something that can be repeated hundreds, thousands of times each day. It's an effort that has to be applied persistently – it cannot be achieved through any short-cuts, which are always based in the use of excessive force in the moment.

The consistent use of too much effort in meditation is always rooted in self-concern. It is typified by an attitude of worry about 'my practice', 'my progress' or 'my lack of progress'.

Another of its hallmarks is laziness. This sometimes surprises people but for many trying too hard is the line of least resistance. It is a habit so deeply ingrained that they don't even need to think to do it. It is something they could do (and almost certainly do do) in their sleep. Consistent meditative over-effort is unthinking and blind.

Here we have the paradoxes that most over-effort is based in laziness, and that to overcome such laziness a meditator must stop trying so hard.

The only way of finding the correct balance of energy in the meditation is through mindfulness. Those who do try too hard need to develop mindfulness so that they become able to restrain the use of force in the moment. This restraint itself requires effort, and so they have to use effort to restrain effort. Restraint has a selfish component – it is still an action I do to produce a certain result – but it is a lot less selfish than believing that I can knock the meditation into shape solely through my own efforts now.

Throughout the path we use selfishness to overcome selfishness and craving to overcome craving. The reason the Buddha taught a path is because we cannot just drop all our views and attachments and instantly become enlightened. The path allows us to start where we are. It acknowledges our undisciplined and selfish nature and describes a course of training in which all craving and selfishness can be overcome. But what drives us to follow the path is selfishness and craving. We would never choose to undergo training if we didn't crave to overcome distress.

The path redirects our cravings from the inefficient to the efficient. Instead of craving for riches and fame we crave for mindfulness, insight, compassion, enlightenment. When this craving has led to the development of a trained mind, one from which all aspects of coarse selfishness have been removed, then it is possible that there will be the subtlety of mind present which is necessary for the total transcendence of craving.

When people accuse meditators of being selfish, spending all that time working at their own spiritual development, on one level they are right, for the attempt to become enlightened is always going to contain some idea of myself. At the same time it is also the most unselfish action it is possible to perform, infinitely less selfish than not treading the spiritual path.

We have to do the work by ourselves, for ourselves, but we also have to remember that an important part of the path is increasing our concern for others.

Some Buddhist writers have denigrated the Theravada path, calling it a lesser vehicle, especially when compared with the Mahayana path. Within the Mahayana tradition, the development of compassion and concern for others is more explicitly emphasised but, whichever path one follows, there has to be a balance between one's own personal meditation and service to others.

Working exclusively for others is an extreme and, from the point of view of coming to enlightenment, it is as unhelpful as being obsessed with one's own practice.

A path that uses craving to overcome craving, selfishness to overcome selfishness, a path that doesn't produce enlightenment but without which enlightenment is not possible, is inescapably paradoxical.

So where does this leave us? It shows us that the path is far too subtle and multi-levelled ever to be reduced to rules or dogma. It shows us that we won't get anywhere without mindfulness and intelligence. It shows that we cannot take things for granted, and that we shouldn't believe our expectations.

Paradoxically, we need both to be more serious about the path and to have a much lighter touch.

The Buddha's Last Journey

May 1995

*'Haven't I always said that it is in the nature of those
things most near and dear to us that we must divide
ourselves from them, leave them, sever ourselves from them?
How could it be that something born, become, compounded,
should not die?'*

Mahaparinibbana Suttanta

The Buddha's Last Journey

'Come, Ananda, let us go to Kusinara.' With these words the Buddha's last journey began. He was eighty years old and had already declared that soon he would die.

From the *Mahaparinibbana Suttanta*, sometimes translated as 'The Book of the Great Decease', we learn a great deal about the Buddha's last few months. In fact, his last year is one of the best documented periods of his whole life.

The *sutta* begins in Rajagaha, where a king was considering doing what kings were very fond of - attacking a neighbouring state. The king sent his minister to the Buddha to find out if his plan would succeed. The Buddha said that it would not, for those he wished to destroy lived in such a way that their prosperity and welfare were guaranteed. The Buddha then called the monks together and taught them how they should live so that the success and welfare of the order would be assured.

As is recorded so often in the Canon, the Buddha turned a situation around and used it as an opportunity to teach.

Perhaps one of the most striking things we learn from the *Mahaparinibbana Suttanta* is the sheer amount of teaching the Buddha did. He was eighty years old, in failing health, travelling everywhere on foot, and yet he delivered discourse after discourse to communities of monks, nuns and lay people, not to mention all the personal instruction he gave to individuals. Thus he spent the last year of his life, just as he had spent all the other years since he first proclaimed the noble truths at Sarnath, forty-four years previously.

The *sutta* details his travels from Rajagaha to Kusinara. Usually accompanied by a large group of monks, he visited Ambalatthika, Nalanda, Pataligama, Kotigama - in all, over a dozen different locations at each of which he taught.

The *sutta* summarises many of these discourses as follows: 'This is ethics, this is concentration, this is wisdom. Concentration, when imbued with ethics, brings great fruit and profit. Wisdom, when imbued with concentration, brings great fruit and profit. The mind imbued with wisdom becomes completely free from the *asava* - that is, the *asava* of sensuality, of becoming, of views and of ignorance.' Or sometimes he focused specifically on the importance of the precepts.

Wherever he taught, to those well-established on the path or to those coming to it for the first time, his purpose was always the same. The Buddha taught for only one reason: the overcoming of distress. One individual might be instructed in keeping the precept of not indulging in intoxicants, another might be instructed in the finer points of meditation. Whichever, the result is the same: the reduction of *dukkha*.

At Ambalatthika, Sariputta told the Buddha that it was clear to him that there never had been nor ever would be a teacher who was better or more enlightened than Gotama himself. For saying which, Sariputta, himself enlightened and the senior disciple, was reprimanded. The Buddha pointed out that Sariputta knew nothing of the minds of the Buddhas of the past or the future, and thus his comments were pure speculation.

The life of the Buddha, devoted to teaching the way to enlightenment, shows us the very highest expression of compassion. That compassion includes the correction and disciplining of those under instruction or those representing the teaching. In this case, the Buddha reprimanded Sariputta, not wanting the *dhamma* to be tainted with untruths, no matter how well-meant.

At a village called Nadika, Ananda asked the Buddha about the rebirths of a long list of lay people who had recently died. (I'm sure things would be just the same if the Buddha had lived today; it's not hard to imagine certain sections of the community pressing the Buddha to publish league tables of meditators' attainments.)

The Buddha told Ananda exactly how far along the spiritual path these people had advanced and in what state they would be reborn. But he went on to say that he found such questions tiresome. He said it was much better if meditators came to know through their own experience that *nibbana* was assured.

Moving on to Vesali, the Buddha stayed in a grove belonging to the courtesan Ambapali. After listening to a discourse she invited the Buddha and the order of monks to accept a meal on the following day.

A little later a group of nobles arrived who also invited the Buddha to a meal. When the Buddha told them he had already accepted an invitation, they approached Ambapali and offered her a considerable sum of money to let them give the meal instead. She replied that she wouldn't give it up for all the kingdom.

The Buddha taught for the sake of all beings. He taught and accepted gifts from rich and poor alike. He was the true revolutionary to whom social status meant nothing. Within the order, the social caste background of the members meant nothing. A former slave would be senior to a former prince if the slave had been ordained earlier. And the Buddha, having agreed to accept a meal from a courtesan, would not subsequently change his mind to avoid upsetting royal supporters. To the Buddha, a noble was not someone with high caste birth, riches or secular power but someone established on the path to truth.

During the rainy season, the Buddha stayed at Vesali, where he became seriously ill. But he resolved that he would not die without having first taken formal leave of the order. At the thought of the Buddha's imminent death, Ananda was very distressed, but he reassured himself by thinking that the Buddha would not die without giving instructions about the future of the order.

On hearing this, the Buddha said that no such instructions needed to be given; he had taught *dhamma*, the way to truth was laid down. He told Ananda that he should rely on nothing but *dhamma* and that the way to do that was to practise the four foundations of mindfulness. The Buddha said, 'Either now or when I am gone, it is those, whoever they may be, who make *dhamma* their refuge, who will be foremost among my followers.'

After this, the Buddha and Ananda spent a day at the Capala Shrine. Here the Buddha told Ananda that anyone who had developed the psychic powers to perfection could, through the exercise of volition, decide to prolong their life and live for the fullest possible human lifespan; in other words they could choose to live until they were in the region of a hundred years old. He added that he himself possessed those psychic powers. Ananda was silent.

The Buddha repeated his statement a second and then a third time, but still Ananda said nothing. Later that day there was a great earthquake. Ananda went to the Buddha and enquired about its cause.

The Buddha explained that there were various physical causes of earthquakes, there were psychic causes and there were also earthquakes associated with events in the life of a Buddha - when the being destined to become Buddha is conceived, when he is born, when he becomes Buddha, when he starts to teach, when he decides to die and when he finally does die.

The Buddha told Ananda how once, soon after his enlightenment, Mara had visited him and suggested that the time was right for the Buddha to die. The Buddha replied that he would not do so until there were monks, nuns, lay men and lay women who were fully trained and established in *dhamma* and who could teach what they themselves had learned.

The Buddha went on to say that Mara had now visited once more and again suggested that he should die. This time the Buddha told him not to worry, for in three months' time his life would indeed come to an end.

Hearing this, Ananda beseeched the Buddha to use his psychic powers to remain alive for a longer period, but the Buddha said that the time for such requests was past. Ananda had had the opportunity and had let it slip.

The Buddha described his body as worn out, like an old cart held together with straps, and said it was only when he was deeply concentrated that he could escape from physical pain. He might have prolonged his life, but the right conditions had not been present. And after all, his way to truth had been successfully established and now flourished. He had achieved that which he had set out to.

The Buddha continued to teach, spending his last few weeks travelling to various communities of monks. At Pava he accepted a meal from Cunda the blacksmith, a meal containing the contaminated food which brought on his final attack of dysentery. From there, weakened and dying, he set out to walk the last few miles to Kusinara. On the way he was given two robes made from gold thread, one which he accepted for himself, one which he requested should be presented to Ananda.

When the golden robe material was placed next to the Buddha's skin, Ananda exclaimed that the Buddha's skin was so radiant that, in comparison, the gold cloth looked quite dull. The Buddha said that there were two occasions on which the colour of the skin of the Tathagata (the term the Buddha always used when referring to himself) becomes clear and exceedingly bright: on the day of his enlightenment and on the day of his death.

'And now this day, Ananda,' he said, 'at the third watch of the night, in the Upavattana of Kusinara, in the sal grove of the Mallians, between the twin sal trees, the utter passing away of the Tathagata will take place.'

The Buddha then bathed in the River Kakuttha and spoke to Ananda concerning Cunda. He said that no one should make Cunda feel guilty for having served him his final meal. He said that, far from being anything to feel remorseful about, giving the Tathagata his final meal was an extraordinarily meritorious action, one that would bring Cunda great good fortune.

Then the Buddha, Ananda and a large number of monks made their way to the sal grove. The Buddha said, 'Ananda, prepare me a bed between these twin sal trees with my head to the north. I am weary and would lie down.' The Buddha lay down on his right side in the lion-posture, mindful and self-possessed.

The *sutta* tells us how the sal trees came into flower even though it was the wrong season, and of various other strange phenomena that occurred around the Buddha's deathbed. The Buddha had to tell one monk who was fanning him to step aside for he was blocking the view of countless devas who had come to pay their respects to the dying Buddha.

At one point the Buddha noticed that Ananda had disappeared and asked where he had gone. A monk told him that Ananda had returned to his lodging and was weeping and saying that he was not yet enlightened and now his teacher was dying, his teacher who had always been so kind.

The Buddha called Ananda to him and told him not to be distressed. 'Haven't I always said that it is in the nature of those things most near and dear to us that we must divide ourselves from them, leave them, sever ourselves from them? How could it be that something born, become, compounded, should not die? For a long time,

Ananda, you have been very near to me, showing *metta* in acts of body, speech and mind. You have done well, Ananda. Be earnest in effort, and you too shall soon be free of the *asava*.'

A little later, the Buddha sent Ananda into Kusinara to inform the townspeople that that very night the Tathagata would die. The townspeople, it's said, were 'grieved, and sad, and afflicted at heart. And some of them wept, tearing their hair, and fell to the ground in anguish at the thought, "Too soon will the Exalted One die, too soon will the light of the world vanish away".'

Staying in Kusinara was a wanderer called Subhadda who, on hearing the news of the Buddha's imminent death, decided that he must try to see him. He approached Ananda, requesting an audience. Ananda said no, telling him the Buddha was too tired. The Buddha overheard their conversation and said that he would talk to Subhadda, and he taught him the true path to enlightenment.

Subhadda knew he had at last found the way to truth and there and then requested ordination. The Buddha directed Ananda to receive him into the order and, 'from immediately after his ordination, the venerable Subhadda remained alone and separate, earnest, zealous and resolute, and before long he attained to that supreme goal of the meditative life'.

Finally, the Buddha addressed the monks, saying that perhaps some of them had doubts or uncertainties about *dhamma* or the training; if they did, then now was the time to ask. There were no questions. All of those present were so well-trained that they had left all doubts behind.

The Buddha then spoke his final words: 'Decay is inherent in all conditioned things. Strive on with diligence.' He withdrew into deep meditation and died.

Afterword

Between his enlightenment and his death the Buddha taught
many, many people, starting with his first five disciples and
ending with Subhadda. Many of those taught, and in turn
many of their pupils taught, and so it continued. Thus
countless teaching lineages all trace their origin back to the
discourses of the Buddha himself.

So, from the twin sal trees of Kusinara, how did the
teaching come down to us here at the House of Inner
Tranquillity? After the Buddha's death, the dhamma spread
throughout northern India. After some two hundred years, by
the time of the reign of Asoka, it had become established as the
popular religion. Asoka sent out various emissaries to spread
the teaching. One of the destinations was what we now know
as Thailand.

In India interest in the teaching slowly waned until it was
dealt its final death-blow round about 1,200 CE by Islamic
invaders. But by that time Thailand and south-east Asia had
become the heartland of Theravadin Buddhism. Over the
centuries many Thai monks perfected their understanding of
the dhamma, keeping alive the path to enlightenment.

Towards the end of last century, a man was born who was
to become Cassandaro Bhikkhu. He too perfected his
meditation and began to teach. His reputation spread and his
monastery, Wat Paknam, attracted monks not only from
Thailand but from neighbouring countries as well. It also
attracted a man from London, William Purfurst. After intensive
meditative training Kapilavaddho, as he had by then become,
was sent back to England to teach.

Kapilavaddho taught Alan and Jacqui James, who went on

to found the House of Inner Tranquillity. Thus there is an
unbroken thread that goes all the way back to the Buddha
himself.

On a global scale, Buddhism is in decline as it has been for
hundreds of years, a decline that has accelerated over the last
few decades with much of traditional Buddhist culture
destroyed. But within this decline there are still occasional
individuals who realise the highest truth of dhamma and
proclaim it to others, such that the teaching remains as pristine
and dynamic as ever.

Alan James has been teaching for over twenty-five years and is
vastly experienced in the way westerners approach the teaching.
There are now many different Buddhist traditions present in the
West but it is our great good fortune to have found a teacher who
teaches the complete path to enlightenment, nothing more, nothing
less.

At Wesak it seems especially appropriate to remember that
the teaching has only survived because of the kindness of
teachers, the kindness that Alan shows us today, the kindness
of Jacqui James, of Kapilavaddho, of his teacher and of his
teacher before him - the same kindness the Buddha showed
Ananda on the night he died.

From that full moon night in May all those centuries ago to
this very moment, dhamma has survived. None of us knows
what the future holds but, in a very real sense, every time we
apply ourselves to the teaching, every time we observe
transience in the moment, we are helping to ensure the
continuation of the Buddha's peerless teaching.

Other books available from Aukana

THE UNFOLDING OF WISDOM
The Buddha's Path to Enlightenment

Alan James

' … *it is like having lived all your life in a dark cave, never being sure where the walls, the ceiling or the exits were, never being sure of the real shape of the space around you. When at last you bring in some light to the darkness, immediately your old idea of the cave disappears. The illumination of true vision eliminates what had been total darkness, including all your speculations about the reality of the cave.*

'*When this occurs, there is never any need to refer to your earlier idea of how things were; it simply becomes irrelevant. Now you know things as they are. What interest can speculative fantasies have for you now?*'

The Unfolding of Wisdom is uncompromising. It presents the facts about spiritual progress. It is not for those who would speculate about symbolism or metaphor but for those who would dare to approach truth directly.

ISBN   0 9511769 4 3 (hardback)
       0 9511769 5 1 (softback)
230 x 155mm   224 pages

MODERN BUDDHISM

Alan & Jacqui James

'The Buddha's teaching is as relevant today as it ever has been. It describes the facts of human life which are observable by anyone who cares to take the trouble to investigate.'

Presenting timeless truths in a 20th-century context, *Modern Buddhism* provides answers to questions that have always haunted mankind.

Death and dying: a wasted and terrifying experience - or an opportunity for spiritual growth? A meditation teacher describes the way she helped her mother approach the doors of death.

Family relationships: why do some families live in harmony, whilst others are constantly at war? What is the purpose of the family unit?

Sexuality: what sexual habits are most conducive to progress along the path?

Alan & Jacqui James belong to the tradition of teachers who present the essence of Buddhism in a way which is totally in tune with the needs of their own time and culture.

In a confused and dark world, the book is like a ray of light showing the path to sanity and peace - **Buddhism Today, Brisbane**

ISBN 0 9511769 1 9
215 x 135mm   176 pages

BUDDHIST CHARACTER ANALYSIS

Robert Mann & Rose Youd

Food, sleep, relationships, sex: do you go for quality, quantity or moderation? Or would you prefer to live without them?

Buddhist Character Analysis is a practical guide to the infinite complexities of human behaviour.

You're offered your own TV show. Do you think, 'What took them so long?' Or would you rather die?

Based exclusively on observable facts, **Buddhist Character Analysis** identifies our fundamental motives and assumptions.

Does your heart sink at the prospect of a quiet weekend? Or do you believe that the world could be a wonderful place if it wasn't for all those people?

Skilful use of **Buddhist Character Analysis** leads to a greater understanding of human nature and increasing happiness in daily life.

How do you see the enlightened person? An aloof Himalayan hermit, master of self-control? Or a charismatic leader using his powers to create a better world?

Combined with a spiritual training, **Buddhist Character Analysis** deepens insight into the true nature of reality.

ISBN 0 9511769 3 5
197 x 125mm   144 pages

LIFE AS A SIAMESE MONK

Richard Randall

May 1954, Bangkok – 10,000 people converge on the outlying temple of Wat Paknam to witness an historic ceremony. 47-year-old journalist Richard Randall is taking the saffron robe to ordain as a Buddhist monk. Known henceforth as Kapilavaddho Bhikkhu, he is the first Englishman to enter the monkhood in Thailand. After an intensive meditation training and some remarkable experiences in concentration and insight practice, Kapilavaddho later went on to play a key role in the introduction of Buddhist meditation to the West.

An exceptionally fine Dhamma-read - **Buddhism Now**

An inspiring story of Buddhist devotion -
Light of Peace, Bangkok

ISBN 0 9511769 2 7
230 x 150mm   224 pages + 8 pages b/w photographs

These books are available by mail order:

Buddhism in a Foreign Land	£8.50
The Unfolding of Wisdom	
softback	£8.95
hardback	£10.95
Modern Buddhism	£7.95
Buddhist Character Analysis	£6.95
Life as a Siamese Monk	£8.95

(Prices include postage and packing)

Please send to:

Aukana Trust
9 Masons Lane
Bradford on Avon
Wiltshire BA15 1QN